PLANNING
AND
UNDERSTANDING

A Computational Approach to Human Reasoning

PLANNING
AND
UNDERSTANDING

A Computational Approach to Human Reasoning

Robert Wilensky

University of California, Berkley

1983

Addison-Wesley Publishing Company
Advanced Book Program
Reading, Massachusetts

London • Amsterdam • Don Mills, Ontario • Sydney • Tokyo

Library of Congress Cataloging in Publication Data

Wilensky, Robert, 1951–
    Planning and understanding.

    (The Addison-Wesley series in artificial intelligence)
    Bibliography: p. 157
    Includes indexes.
    1. Reasoning (Psychology)   2. Problem solving.
3. Psycholinguistics.   4. Artificial intelligence.
I. Title.   II. Series.
BF441.W53   1983   001.53'5   82-16367
ISBN 0-201-09590-4

Manufactured in the United States of America

BCDEFGHIJ–MA–898765432

TABLE OF CONTENTS

Preface

CONTENTS

This book brings together two areas of cognition: common-sense problem solving, and natural language understanding. To do so, three theoretical notions are presented: a theory of plan generation, a theory of plan-based understanding, and a theory of the structure of plans that underlies both theories of processing. Each of the three theories influences the shape of the others, and this interaction is partially responsible for the way in which these theories differ from previous efforts.

This work began as a study of the inference procedures required for natural language text understanding. This portion of the research, begun at the Yale Artificial Intelligence Project and continued at Berkeley Artificial Intelligence Research Project of the University of California, led to the development of the theory of plan-based understanding, and its incorporation in a computer program called PAM (Plan Applier Mechanism). Beginning with an approach to text understanding developed by Roger Schank and Robert Abelson, my attempt to construct a text understander led to the conclusion that existing theories of plan structure were insufficient to account for the richness of commonplace situations. Subsequent research, which constituted my doctoral dissertation, was largely concerned with developing the more complex planning structures required for this task. Those readers familiar wih my dissertation will recognize the reappearance of much of it here.

The inability of a theory of plans to account for common-sense situations means that the theory will also be too weak to account for a planner's ability to create a reasonable course of action in such situations. Similarly, if my extended theory improves the state of the computational understander, it should also improve the state of the plan generator. Thus I applied the theory to planning in common-sense situations. As might be expected, the more complex planning structures required a different planning model than had been developed previously. The resulting model and its incorporation in a computer program called PANDORA (Plan ANalysis with Dynamic Organization, Revision, and Application) figures prominently in this book.

In addition, the development of this model of plan generation caused me to recast some of my original theory of plan structure in a quite different framework. Much of the analysis presented in my previous work is still apparent here, but many technical issues now appear to be resolved and many loose ends have been tied. The recast theory of plan structure constitutes the bulk of this work.

Revision of the theory of plans also led to a revision of the theory of understanding. Although these changes did not undermine major theoretical assumptions, they did eventually engender a completely different implementation of the understanding mechanism. Drawbacks of the previous implementations are discussed along with the details of the current programs in the final chapters.

STRATEGY

Artificial Intelligence is a field renowned for its lack of consensus on fundamental issues. As one proceeds from Artificial Intelligence to the more ill-defined field of Cognitive Science, common ground becomes an even scarcer resource. Much of the research related to cognition is not accepted as valid by colleagues nurtured in other traditions; the subjective appraisal of the importance of a contribution is subject to even wider differences of opinion.

The research represented by this book is not likely to be an exception. The primary purpose of the work is to facilitate the Artificial Intelligence goal of producing more intelligent devices. However, the methodology entails an inquiry into the structure of human behavior. The research thus makes claims about human psychology, computer modeling, and cognition in general. As one of the concerns of this work is natural language understanding, the theories present impinge upon the domain of the linguist as well. To cater to such a diverse audience is most likely an impossible task, and therefore has not been attempted by this author. Even the narrower goal of making this research accessible to that body of computer scientists, cognitive psychologists, and discourse-oriented linguists concerned with cognitive processes has required some compromises.

Artificial Intelligence researchers, for example, may be dismayed at the lack of explicit description of computer programs as an accompaniment to the theoretical exposition. While the description of such programs is given in some detail in the final chapters, I felt that its inclusion would detract more from the theoretical development than it would illuminate it. Partly this is because the implementation details required for this presentation are largely beside the point. While efficient implementations are certainly an important goal for computer scientists, including this author, they do not in themselves constitute a significant part of the theories being presented.

The risk entailed by this decision, of course, is that the presentation may leave unanswered questions in a reader's mind as to how a theory presented might be realized, if it is realizable at all, or if the attempt to implement it might reveal the theory to be only a trivial variant of some previous theory. These concerns are quite real, and are only exacerbated by the fact that, in many cases, the implementation has lagged behind the theoretical development. The inclusion of a separate section of implementation details is an attempt to alleviate this problem, but to some degree the problem is inherent in a work of this kind.

Cognitive psychologists might take objection to the lack of reference to the experimental literature, or with the failure to bolster my claims with experimental evidence. The first point reflects more my general finding that the experimental literature is not as helpful as I would like rather than a bias against such work. I attribute this mostly to the lack of a sufficiently strong theoretical foundation from which such results would be most useful. As the goal of this work is to supply some of this foundation, empirical explorations that could be related to it would most likely be illuminating. It would be gratifying if this book serves to prompt such investigations.

Traditional psychological evidence being neglected and computer simulations providing only partial support, most of the arguments used to substantiate the theories offered herein are logical analyses abstracted from numerous examples. This methodology often leaves unanswered questions about the completeness of an analysis and runs the risk of being overly pedantic. However, it seems to me that this methodology has given rise to new ideas and insights, and provides tentative support for them. Incomplete as the work may be, I feel strongly enough about the value of these ideas and their supporting evidence to warrant their publication at this time.

ACKNOWLEDGEMENT

While the research reported in this book is my own, it is also the product of many seminars and informal discussions with my previous advisors, colleagues, and current students. Certainly, the guidance of my former advisor Roger Schank is responsible for the initial direction this research took; the work of Schank and Abelson is a notable influence throughout. Numerous interactions with the members of the Yale Artificial Intelligence Project no doubt resulted in many contributions to my work.

Many of the ideas upon which this book is based derive from interactions among the members of BAIR, the Berkeley Artificial Intelligence Research Project. The following students often contributed important insights that directly advanced the state of our work: Yigal Arens, Margaret Butler, David Chin, Robert Coyne, Michael Deering, Joe Faletti, Tom Hahn, Robert Holt, Paul Jacobs, Marc Luria, James Martin, James Mayfield, Fred Mueller, Peter Norvig, Lisa Rau, and Steve Upstill.

In addition, a number of these students are responsible for the programs I describe. Michael Deering and Peter Norvig developed the more recent implementations of PAM; in particular, Peter Norvig has worked on the frame-based version described in Chapter 12. Joe Faletti is responsible for the current version of PANDORA. Both Faletti and Norvis have worked on the representation of plans in these programs, and have contributed directly to the ideas described in Chapters 11 and 12. PEARL, a programming language in which these programs are implemented, was written by Michael Deering and Joe Faletti. Marc Luria has written the most recent question answering system that runs in conjunction with PAM; Steve Upstill and Paul Jacobs developed the current natural language generator.

The portion of this research done at Yale was supported by the Advanced Research Projects Agency of the Department of Defense, and monitored by the Office of Naval Research under contract N00014-75-C-1111. At Berkeley, this work was supported in part by the Office of Naval Research under contract N00014-80-C-0732 and by the National Science Foundation under grant MCS 79-06543.

Robert Wilensky

PLANNING AND UNDERSTANDING

A Computational Approach to Human Reasoning

1

Introduction

1.1 APPROACHES TO COGNITION

How do people understand natural language? How do they behave rationally in a variety of situations? How can computers be made to do likewise?

These are some of the central questions at the intersection of a number of fields: artificial intelligence, cognitive psychology, and linguistics. The researcher in artificial intelligence is interested in extending the capabilities of computer systems to encompass natural language use and common-sense reasoning capabilities. This has led to concern about the methods humans use to perform these tasks, traditionally the domain of the cognitive psychologist. Similarly, psychologists interested in human cognitive capacities have found the computer a convenient tool, both because it provides a vocabulary for talking about cognitive processes and because it requires a precision in developing theories which forces the theorist to confront problems that may not show up otherwise.

Linguists, too, have recently come to be concerned with the mechanisms involved in language use, particularly in the area of text linguistics. As linguists increasingly involve themselves with the study of meaningful natural language tasks rather than with the analysis of isolated structural components, their attention has turned to the interactions of linguistic knowledge with nonlinguistic knowledge. Thus the artificial intelligence researcher's goal of building systems that perform meaningful natural language tasks begins to converge with the linguist's goal of studying language in realistic contexts.

At the present time, there is at least as much to separate these fields as there is to bring them together. What they do have in common is a concern about the knowledge required for intelligent behavior. It has become axiomatic to most computer scientists that no intelligent system can be constructed unless it employs large quanitites of world knowledge. Psychologists, by the nature of their field, are compelled to be concerned with the structure of knowledge in the human mind, and linguists, with the knowledge people have that enables them to use language as an instrument of communication.

Thus a unifying thread in the cognitive sciences is the need to explore the nature of knowledge: how it can be represented, how it can be stored and accessed, and how it can be used in the various tasks thought to constitute cognition.

The purpose of this book is to ask such questions about two areas of cognition: planning and understanding. Planning concerns the process by which people select a course of action—deciding what they want, formulating and revising plans, dealing with problems and adversity, making choices, and eventually performing some action. Understanding concerns the way in which a person comprehends a situation—inferring implicit components, establishing coherence of an episode, structuring events into meaningful units, and finding explanations for other people's actions.

The analysis presented here does not pretend to be complete. However, as some parts of the theory are worked out in detail, this book provides a concrete model of at least some parts of the topics just mentioned. Moreover, it suggests an approach for rectifying the sins of ommission perpetrated herein. This book has accomplished its objective if the reader can determine not only what the theory claims, but where it can be painlessly extended or modified and, more importantly, where it cannot.

1.2 ASSUMPTIONS, VIEWPOINTS, AND METHODOLOGY

Some caveats are in order about the kind of theory I seek. As this work claims some relevance to human psychology, the reader may wonder what scientific means have been used to test this theory. For example, has the traditional arsenal of the psychologist been used to perform experiments on human subjects, demonstrating the plausibility of my claims? By and large, it has not. While such experiments would be a welcome supplement, I do not believe their impact would be particularly significant at this time. The reason for this is that my approach to cognition has not been in the form of the question usually posed by psychology, namely, "Exactly what do humans do?" but rather, "How is cognition possible in the first place?" Psychological experimentation has been successful at establishing many fine details about the nature of particular human cognitive functions, but it has been less successful at answering important questions about the status of these facts, such as which of them are crucial to the performance of the task in question, which of them are artifacts of more fundamental processes, and which of them might just as well have been otherwise.

The methodology used in this research has been to make an inquiry into what might be termed the *architecture of cognition*. By this I mean an examination of the tasks themselves, with an emphasis on what must be done to accomplish them, regardless of the mechanisms employed. Thus a major portion of this book is devoted to dissecting the problem—dividing it into subcategories, analyzing the information and processes needed for each component, and dealing with the consequences of having such components and the representations they entail in an integrated system. In this methodology, such an examination is accompanied by a projection of these requirements into constraints on the possible processing models and knowledge representations that could support such a task. Finally, concrete proposals for the actual mechanisms are given.

The intention in most cases is for these concrete proposals to be just abstract enough to capture the essential nature of what it means to perform a certain task, without being so abstract as to make no commitments at all. While there is no guarantee that the mechanisms offered here are the ones people use, it seems to me that those mechanisms could not differ from the ones suggested here in important ways unless some error has been made in the analysis. Of course, this is not a defense of my theories, which in fact may suffer from such errors, but rather one of the methodology employed. Essentially the methodology consists of examining a large number of hypothetical situations thought to be instances of the task in question, extracting the requirements from each one, building these into a model, applying the model to more situations for continued refinement, and finally, iterating this process with highly detailed computer simulations.

This process bears a resemblance to that used in certain parts of linguistics. However, there is one important difference. Here I am concerned with studying a large number of diverse factors that contribute to a definable and valid cognitive task, whereas much of linguistics has used this methodology to study theoretical constructs meaningful only within the confines of the theory. The primary goal of my approach is the elucidation of cognitive processes along with the knowledge that they employ, thereby bettering the odds that our theories will actually be relevant to human activity.

Current models in the cognitive sciences are relatively impoverished. We do not have, as in the physical sciences, several highly developed theories, each capable of describing a vast array of phenomena and differing only in minute, detailed predictions about extremely exotic events. Rather, we have only faint ideas about how the most basic aspects of cognition could be accomplished at all, let alone how precisely people do these. Considering the current status of our understanding of cognition, I feel that the approach to cognition adopted here is appropriate.

1.2.1 Programs and Theories

A problem that plagues computer scientists who wish to develop cognitive models is the relationship of programs to theories. In particular, the question arises as to which parts of a program are meant to be taken seriously, and for the ones that are, what is the correspondence between the program and the theory. In my own case, the answer is derived from the goals of my research. The aim is to present an architecture for a program—a description abstract to capture the essential nature of a process, but concrete enough so that its realization can be easily envisioned (in fact, a particular implementation is provided).

Consider the following analogy. Computer architects often talk about three levels of description of a computer: its architecture, its implementation, and its realization. The architecture is a functional description of how the machine appears to the programmer—what each of instructions does, how much memory it can access, whether it uses a hardware stack, and so on. Its implementation is a logical design that supports that architecture. Thus the logical design may include a second program counter used to speed things up internally, but of which the programmer is never aware. The realization is the physical design of the machine—the particular components obtained from a manufacturer to assemble the actual device. Thus a single architecture can be supported by any number of different implementations, each of which may have numerous realizations. In fact, it is often the case that the same architecture is realized in newer technologies as they become available.

The theories I seek here are closest to architectures in nature. As such, I mean for them to be taken quite literally. However, they are generally well removed from the particular program implementation provided. In most cases, such implementations are more a means of determining the plausibility and consistency of the theory than they are a crucial part of the theory per se. Indeed, the functional descriptions included here do not entail a commitment to either parallel or serial implementation, or to any number of other choices that must be made before a particular realization can be effected.

Of course, there is a separate issue of whether such isolatable levels actually can be found for the mind. The presumption that some such meaningful levels do exist seems to be basic not only in artificial intelligence, but to all of cognitive science. Although this assumption has been called into question recently from philosophical quarters (e.g., Dreyfus, 1972; Searle, 1981), I know of no way to evaluate it other than to carry out the cognitive science research program to which it gives rise. This work may be viewed as such an effort.

1.3 PLANNING, UNDERSTANDING, AND THE THEORY OF PLANS

This book addresses some issues that arise in attempts to construct theories of planning and of understanding. Here a theory of planning means an account of how people decide what actions to take in a given situation; a theory of understanding is concerned with how people construct explanations to account for the actions of others. The following example indicates the scope of these concerns and the general goals of this research.

Consider this example of planning. A person realizes that a friend's birthday is coming up and decides to go to the drugstore to buy that friend a birthday card. To understand how someone arrives at this rather straightforward course of action, we must account for a number of cognitive processes. First, the individual must assess the situation to come to have a goal. That is, the person must realize that this event is approaching, and that celebrating it is therefore in order. Having this goal, the person now must determine a way to fulfill it. In this case, the standard plan of sending a birthday card is chosen. To carry out this plan, the planner must recognize that certain preconditions must exist, namely, that he must have a card to send. A plan to achieve this condition is generated, resulting in the planner's decision to buy a card, and subsequently, to go to the drugstore for this purpose.

Thus planning includes assessing a situation, deciding what goals to pursue, creating plans to secure these goals, and executing plans. Consider now what is involved in comprehension. Suppose we were told a sequence of events such as those mentioned at the beginning of the preceding paragraph: someone realizes that a friend's birthday is approaching and decides to go to the drugstore to buy a birthday card. As the receivers of this information, we are faced with the task of making sense out of it. To do so, we must come to a number of realizations both about the events explicitly described and some events not mentioned at all. For example, we must realize that the person buying the card intended to send it to the person whose birthday was approaching, and that he was doing so because he wanted to acknowledge the happy occasion. These items are not actually mentioned in the description of the situation, but we could not be said to have really understood this situation unless we assumed that they were in fact the case.

Understanding a situation entails realizing that explicitly mentioned events are part of a reasonable plan for a goal. For example, going to a drugstore in the preceding example must be understood as part of a plan for sending someone a birthday card. Had it not been interpreted as such, the situation would have made as much sense as if we were told that someone decided to celebrate a friend's birthday by wearing an old coat.

Thus understanding a situation involves inferring the goals, plans, and actions of the people in that situation, and relating these items to each other as well as to other aspects of the situation. On the surface, these tasks appear to have little in common with the tasks that constitute planning—choosing one's own goals and generating plans for them. However, what is common to planning and understanding is that both require recourse to essentially the same sort of knowledge about plans. An example of such knowledge is that buying an item is a way of obtaining possession of that item. This fact is used in the planning example to suggest the plan of buying a birthday card once the need to obtain one has been established. This fact is also used in the understanding example. Here, however, it is used to help infer that someone is going to send a card to someone, having learned of the intention to purchase one.

Although understanding and planning are quite different processes, they both require an understanding of the structure and content of planning knowledge. Both need to know that plans are used to achieve goals, and what plans are good for what goals; that certain situations give rise to goals under certain circumstances, and what particular goals, situations, and circumstances are related; that events can affect the outcome of goals, and what kinds of events affect what kinds of goals; and that goals can interact with one another, and what particular kinds of interactions there are.

The structure and content of this knowledge is referred to here as the *theory of plans.* It is the major concern of this work. As such, I will examine this knowledge in great detail from the perspectives of both planning and understanding, a primary goal of the endeavor being to formulate this knowledge in a fashion suitable for both purposes.

In addition to the central underlying concern of a theory of plans, I am also interested in the processes that make use of the declarative knowledge described by this theory, that is, the processes of planning and understanding. Thus there are three theories to develop:

1. *The theory of planning, which describes the process by which an intelligent agent determines and executes a plan of action.*

2. *The theory of understanding, which describes the process by which an understander comes to comprehend the behavior of another.*

3. *The theory of plans, which describes the knowledge about planning used for both these tasks.*

One further remark is in order about the theory of understanding that I intend to expound. Theories of understanding are usually associated with natural language processing. The theory presented here is intended to be more general. Namely, the theory should be applicable to situations encountered through media other than language, for example, through films or direct experience. However, most of my experience with this theory has been in the natural language realm, and this is likely to be its most important application. In any case, I maintain that any theory of natural language comprehension would require an understanding of the issues that are of central concern here.

1.4 PREVIOUS APPROACHES

Previous work in acting and understanding that has influenced this research has come out of two traditions. The most obvious influence is that of Schank and Abelson (1977), whose work is primarily concerned with natural language processing. Their approach emphasizes the importance of knowledge structures in understanding coherent texts. These researchers introduced the notion of a script as a way of structuring knowledge about stereotyped situations to constrain the inference proliferation that occurs, for example, in Rieger's system (Rieger,

1975a). The script idea was used by Cullingford (1978) in his SAM (Script Applier Mechanism) program, one of the first natural language story understanding systems.

In addition, Schank and Abelson noted the importance of the role of plans and goals in text understanding. This analysis was used as the basis for an early version of PAM (Plan Applier Mechanism), a story understanding program constructed by this author (Wilensky, 1978). Much of the research presented here is a result of, or in some cases a reaction against, this attempt to build a natural language text understander based on plan application.

There has been less direct influence in the area of planning. In artificial intelligence, the area most closely allied with this is that of problem solving. Most of this work has a quite different character than the approach taken here, for reasons I will examine in more detail later. Primarily, most of this work has been in the area of "robot planning" rather than human problem solving. That is, the goal is not so much a theory of cognition but a program that performs certain tasks efficiently. For example, the SRI work on problem solving (Fikes and Nilsson, 1971; Sacerdoti, 1974) generated a number of interesting systems that solved problems involving a robot, some boxes, and a few rooms connected by doors. A number of MIT projects (e.g., Sussman, 1975) solved problems in a blocks world, again without paying close attention to modeling human behavior. Similarly, a great deal of work has recently appeared on "expert systems" (e.g., Shortliffe, 1974; Duda et al., 1978; Stefik, 1980). Here the emphasis is on extracting knowledge from humans, but applying it in a form that is amenable to the human rather than imitative of one.

Newell and Simon's (1972) seminal work in human problem solving is of course concerned with cognitive issues. They have advocated "means-ends" analysis as the basic problem-solving strategy and control structure. Although the spirit of my work is close to theirs, there is one primary difference, which concerns the nature of the problems I am interested in studying. Newell and Simon chose as problems those things that are truly difficult for people and for which little semantic information is available, for example, manipulating meaningless formal symbols, solving cryptarithmetic problems, and other puzzles.

By contrast, I am interested in how people work out a plan in mundane situations where large quantities of world knowledge are useful, necessary, and available. Examples of such situations would be buying something at the supermarket, deciding whether to go to a movie or out for dinner, or figuring out how to prevent someone else from getting a promotion you want.

Planning in commonplace situations has begun to attract increasing attention. For example, Rieger (1975b) has proposed a set of "common-sense algorithms" for reasoning about everyday physical situations; Hayes-Roth and Hayes-Roth (1979) are concerned with how a person might schedule a day's activities; and Carbonell's (1978) POLITICS program reasons dogmatically about political decisions. On another front, Sacerdoti (1977) and McDermott (1977), while operating in the more traditional problem-solving paradigm, have proposed some powerful approaches to general problem solving. McDermott's work in particular has had an important influence on my conception of planning. In addition, Rieger (1975b), McDermott (1977), and more recently Charniak (1981) put forth the idea that representations for knowledge about problem solving should be usable for tasks such as understanding as well, a theme that plays an important role here.

Carbonell's work is especially relevant as he devotes a major portion of it to planning in competitive situations, a topic for concern in the later chapters of this book. Some of this work was developed in parallel to my own, and the theories bear certain similarities. In any case, it is useful to bear his work in mind when considering my presentation of related matters; explicit contrasts are presented when they are illuminating.

2

Tenets of a Theory of Plans

2.1 PLANNING VERSUS UNDERSTANDING IN MORE DETAIL

The theory of plans to be presented here, and thereby the theories of planning and of understanding, is characterized by several important features. This chapter outlines the distinguishing characteristics of this approach. However, before we begin our exposition, it is useful to compare planning and understanding in some more detail.

Problem-solving programs generally have as their goal the construction of a plan whose execution will bring about a desired state. The domain over which plan construction is performed varies considerably, involving, for example, robots finding their way through rooms (Fikes and Nilsson, 1971; Sacerdoti, 1974); "missionary and cannibals" type problems (Newell and Simon, 1972); electronic circuit design (McDermott, 1977); and program construction (Rich and Shrobe, 1976; Barstow, 1977). The domain over which problem solving can be performed may happen to involve natural language. For example, participating in a conversation and producing an utterance have been viewed as problems in plan construction where the problem is to create an utterance that would satisfy goals involving the transmission of certain contents or intentions (Bruce, 1978; Perrault, Allen, and Cohen, 1978).

While problem solving may involve plan construction over quite different domains, including some linguistic ones, the essential nature of the task is the same: given a goal, create a plan to satisfy it. In contrast, in understanding, quite a different application of plans is found. Here the understander needs to follow the goals and plans of actors in a situation in order to make inferences (Schmidt, Sridharan, and Goodson, 1978; Wilensky, 1978). Rather than actually create a plan, an understander must be able to use knowledge about plans to understand the plan under which someone else is operating.

Although problem solving and understanding both heavily involve the use of plans, it is important to emphasize how different these processes are. Problem solving has often been abstractly characterized as searching through a "solution space" for an answer to some problem. That is, given a goal, a set of operators, and an initial state of the world, the task is to construct a sequence of operators that transforms the initial state into the goal state. Understanding involves just the opposite in terms of what is known and what must be computed. For example, stories often state that a character took some action, from which the reader must infer why he did so and what conditions must have existed for the action to have been taken. That is, the reader is given the "solution," in problem-solving terminology, and must reconstruct the goal and state of the world from it. Rather than searching through solution space for an answer, an understander searches through an "explanation space" to find a set of circumstances that would explain a character's behavior.

This characterization of planning and understanding demonstrates that while explanation finding is related to problem solving, it is neither entailed by it nor dependent on it. A good story understander is not required to be an effective problem solver, nor does a problem solver fulfill the requirements of an explanation mechanism. The tasks that arise in understanding impose different requirements than do any involved in problem solving; some simply have no correlate.

For example, the understanding task may require that a goal be inferred from the occurrence of an action and that the existence of a goal be explained. If an understander were told that John proposed to Mary, the understander would need to infer that John probably has the goal of marrying Mary, and that this goal might have come into existence because John loved her. Most problem solvers do not have the facility to infer goals, or explain where they come from—their purpose is simply to act on goals asserted to them. A problem solver, when told that John wants to marry Mary, might deduce that John should try proposing to Mary. But it could not explain where this goal came from nor could it infer that John has this goal from some action he undertook. Furthermore, the plan that a character chose to use might be an unusual one—one that the reader of the story would not or could not produce for the same situation. A reader must therefore be able to comprehend a character's behavior in terms of a plan that that same reader would not produce itself.

This characterization of the two processes is actually somewhat flawed. In particular, I intend to show that a good problem solver should incorporate some of capabilities that were just attributed to understanding mechanisms. For example, a good planning system should be able to infer its own goals and to infer the goals of others, although most planning programs do not have this property. However, the fact that comprehensive understanding and planning systems may embody components of both understanding and planning mechanisms does not defeat the central tenet that such systems are decomposable into separate understanding and planning components, neither of which is more important than the other.

2.2 THE DOMAIN OF MUNDANE ACTIVITIES

The objective of the theory of plans is to characterize the plans underlying everyday activities. In both plan generation and natural language understanding, these plans play a privileged role if only because they are prevalent in daily life and in ordinary texts. A planning mechanism or language understander must be able to manipulate knowledge about these plans if it is to cope with the majority of situations it will encounter.

These sorts of plans differ from those most commonly studied in Artificial Intelligence (AI) in a number of important ways. To begin with, most of the plans examined in AI problem solving involve just those situations at the limits of a person's ability. For example, games such as chess or cryptarithmetic puzzle solving are interesting precisely because the proper actions are not immediately obvious. In contrast, the kind of plans we will be concerned with are those in which the planning or understanding seems almost automatic and for which people's cognitive processing apparatus appears to be well suited.

However, as we will attempt to demonstrate, these mundane plans generally possess structures that are actually more complicated than those normally associated with difficult problems. Everyday planning may be computationally more tractable, but the planning structure is correspondingly richer. The most important implication of this difference is that the structures and processes we will need to develop for everyday plans will not be derivative of those developed for more exotic problems. Rather, the tasks are different enough so that a great deal of independent machinery will have to be created for our specific needs. Moreover our theory will have to be more sophisticated as the situations we wish to study become structurally more complex.

We illustate the complexities of mundane plans with an example. Consider the following story, both from the point of view of planning and of understanding:

(2- 1)   *John's wife called him at the office and told him that they were all out of milk. John said he would pick some up on the way home from work.*

Let us first consider this example from the point of view of the planner. That is, suppose we are in John's position and just received such a phone call. Suppose further that we live out in the suburbs and that we happen to pass a supermarket on the way home. Assuming that we did not have a pattern of behavior already established for this particular situation, how is it that we might come up with this seemingly simple and effective plan?

To begin with, note that we have to infer a goal, namely, that of having some more milk. The actual example merely mentions the state of being out of milk, and we need to infer that we should have the goal of rectifying this situation. Thus we have to respond to an expected situation by determining a particular goal that it is sensible to have in that situation.

Then a plan for this goal has to be generated. This is actually the simplest part of generating the overall plan of action, because in this case, the plan is the well-known plan of shopping at a store. This plan is simply retrieved from memory, having been previously stored as the appropriate plan for just this sort of goal.

Having proposed using this plan, we must now recognize how this plan will interact with other plans and goals we are entertaining. In this case, the plan for buying milk at the supermarket interacts with our plan for being home at the end of the day. In particular, it is important to consider the plans for these two goals together, otherwise we might generate a plan that is considerably less ideal. For example, we might decide to drive all the way to the store, buy the milk, return to the office, and drive past the store again on the way home. Alternatively, we might end up driving all the way home at the end of the day, and then, having fulfilled our goal of being home, drive back to the supermarket to purchase the milk.

Thus we must detect the interactions between this new goal and our other goals, and then alter both our previous and new plans to accommodate the interactions. Here we interweave the plans for the two goals so that some of the tasks common to both plans are achieved simultaneously. That is, the part of the driving that is common to both plans is scheduled to occur only once.

Note that, in addition to recognizing and responding to this situation, the planner must understand *why* this course of action is a good idea. That is, why is it that a plan that satisfies all one's explicit goals may not be a good enough plan? In this example, we reject such plans because they involve the expenditure of effort or resources that would not otherwise be required. Making a separate trip to the store seems unnecessary, so even though the goal may be achieved this way, we select a more economical way of doing so. A more general way of phrasing this principle is that it is good policy for a planner to try to produce plans that do not waste resources. This policy may be thought of as a kind of abstract goal of the planner. Unlike the more specific goals of getting more milk or being home, this goal of not wasting resources is applicable to all situations in which other goals are involved. It is a general principle to which a planner conforms in making plans for other goals, rather than a goal pursued in its own right.

Let us now consider story (2-1) from the point of view of understanding. Essentially the same knowledge comes into play, although here the reader uses this knowledge to infer the reasonableness of a character's plans, or to fill in missing pieces. For example, a reader recognizes John's plan of stopping at the store on the way home as a way of integrating the plans for two goals. In addition, knowledge about such activities is needed to interpret the meaning of the actual sentences of the text. For example, "pick some up" should be interpreted as "buying," not as "lifting." The reader can make this inference only with knowledge about the plans and goals someone is likely to have in this particular situation.

This example has highlighted a number of facets of the theory of plans of mundane situations. We will now describe these facets in more detail.

2.3 THE NEED TO REASON ABOUT GOALS

The first observation we made was that a planner may have to infer the goal he possesses in a given situation. In general, our theory of mundane plans emphasizes reasoning about goals as opposed to reasoning about methods. In contrast, most AI planning systems do relatively little reasoning about goals and emphasize instead the production of plans. For example, in most such planning systems, goals are simply handed to the planner, often in the form of a problem to be solved. However, an autonomous, common-sense planner must be able to infer its own goals based on its overall mission together with the situation in which it finds itself. Likewise, in text comprehension, the reader must be able to infer the goal of a character in order to arrive at an understanding of that character's actions.

The latter point seems consonant with research on dialogue (e.g., Perrault, Allen, and Cohen, 1978), in which goal analysis is needed to understand the intent behind indirect speech acts. Thus to realize that the utterance "Can you reach the salt?" is a request to pass the salt, the speaker's probable goal of using the salt needs to be inferred by the listener.

As a further example, suppose a robot planner were given the job of maintaining a nuclear reactor. In addition to sustaining the generation of power, the robot may also be in charge of keeping the floors clean, preventing meltdowns, cleaning up dangerous spills, while maintaining itself at the same time. However, most of the time most of these goals are inoperative. For example, the robot need not be concerned with cleaning up a spill until one occurs. Thus it is desirable to build a planner than can recognize one of these situations when it occurs and infer the goal it should have at that time. The robot should infer it has the goal of cleaning up a spill when one occurs, of defending itself and the plant if they are attacked by terrorists, and of replenishing its resources if they are low.

Conventional AI models by and large do not deal with this issue of where goals come from. Rather, the focus is on generating a plan for the goal once it is known. In the real world, at least as much work is involved in determining what one wants to do as in determinng how to do it.

2.4 THE IMPORTANCE OF INTERACTIONS BETWEEN GOALS

While most of the work in conventional planners involves constructing a plan for a single goal, most of the planning involved in everyday situations is primarily concerned with the interactions between goals. That is, planning for individual goals is assumed to be a fairly simple matter, consisting primarily of the straightforward application of rather large quantities of world knowledge. The complexity of planning is attributed to the fact that most situations involve numerous goals that interact in complicated ways. For example, in story (2-1) the plans for the individual goals of being home and having milk were simply "canned" plans associated with these goals. The real work was involved in fusing these two plans together.

Simple as this situation may be, most conventional planners are ill-equipped to handle it. This is because most traditional problem-solving research has been concerned with finding the solution to a single, difficult problem (e.g., finding the winning chess move). By contrast, most everyday problem solving consists of synthesizing solutions to individually simple, but complexly interacting, problems.

To be sure, the problem of interacting plans has long been recognized. For example, the work of Sacerdoti (1977), Sussman (1975), Tate (1975), and Warren (1974) all contain explicit methods for dealing with interactions between plan components. My objection to these approaches is primarily one of emphasis: They do not go far enough in stressing the complexity and significance of interactions in the planning process. My claim is that dealing with interactions should be moved from its secondary status to the primary framework around which the planner is designed, and that doing so will result in a substantially different and more advantageous planning control structure.

To make this point more concrete, consider how interactions between plans are dealt with in Sacerdoti's NOAH (I use Sacerdoti's work because I believe it is a superior example of the class of planning systems with which I wish to contrast my own work). NOAH creates successively more detailed plans for a given goal. At each level of specification, the plan is scrutinized by a collection of *critics*. The result of criticism is a plan network free of some existing or potential problem. The resulting plan is then expanded to include more detail, until primitive executable actions have been specified.

For example, one kind of critic will produce a more constrained plan in which an ambiguity that could conceivably lead to faulty execution is resolved in favor of an error-free alternative. Consider the following example borrowed from Sussman (1975). If NOAH were given the task of putting block A on top of block B on top of block C, it would first produce a plan specifying that A should be moved on top of B and that B should be placed on top of C, but not specifying the order in which these moves should be made. Because in the blocks world, a block with an object on top of it cannot be moved, this plan has a potential problem. Fortunately NOAH has a critic that detects such situations. This critic resolves the problem by adding the constraint that A should be put on top of B only after B has been placed on top of C.

Besides resolving conflicts of this sort, NOAH contains critics that revise plans to eliminate unnecessary steps and critics that cause the planner to backtrack out of an unproductive corner. In addition, the user can add domain-dependent critics to handle problems specific to particular domains.

The rationale for criticism is to keep individual plans simple by not incorporating into them information about what to do in the presence of numerous other plans. Rather, rules about handling interactions are distilled into general procedures (critics) that globally scan the planning network and remedy potential problems. In the case of the blocks example, the plan to stack one block upon another contains only information about the preconditions and postconditions of moving a block. The critic that constrained the overall plan is general to situations in which one action can undo the desired effect of another. Thus the individual, domain-specific plans do not describe what to do in case of an adverse interaction, and the critic is general to all such interactions regardless of the domain.

An examination of the critics contained in NOAH reveals that they only begin to cope with the problem. For example, one kind of critic will remove redundant preconditions from a plan. In one of Sacerdoti's examples, the precondition of getting paint occurs once for each of two goals in a plan, so one of the preconditions is removed. However, in a more realistic world model, this change will not work. Rather, a single new precondition must be created that will not just get paint, but get enough paint for both needs. In general, whether it makes sense to throw away a precondition depends on the exact relation of the precondition to the operation of the plan and requires more complex considerations than NOAH is willing to perform.

The multiple occurrence of a precondition entails many other such considerations. For example, the existence of enough instances of the precondition might change the plan that one would choose to achieve it. Thus, if we had a dozen goals involving paint, merging plan components may also require altering our plan from walking to using a truck, or from painting with a brush to spray painting. Many of the techniques that made NOAH as efficient as it is (for example, its use of a table of multiple effects to detect goal conflicts) is based on critics' predicates being relatively simple conditions. But this situation does not persist when the full complexity of goal interactions is allowed.

In addition, NOAH is only concerned about interactions that occurred within a single plan network. Thus, even if it had sufficiently powerful mechanisms for removing redundancies from a plan, for example, it would still lack a mechanism for noticing interactions if the plans are derived from heretofore unrelated goals. For example, if he needed enough items, the planner in story (2-1) might decide to do his week's shopping while he is at the store. This sort of planning is alien to NOAH, which for all its attention to interactions, still treats planning as the task of producing a single plan for a single goal.

A more subtle problem with NOAH is that it really has no notion of what its critics are doing. For example, a critic that resolves a conflict does so because the plan will not work otherwise. But a critic that removes a redundant step does so in order to be efficient, a consideration that has nothing whatsoever to do with the explicit goal NOAH is trying to achieve. One consequence of this is that the program will not know what to do if a plan component resulting from efficiency considerations conflicts with another plan component. The proper solution requires either abandoning the efficient plan component in order to achieve the initial goal or abandoning the original goal because its value is less than the value of the cost of the inefficient plan. That is, the reason behind the action suggested by a critic must be examined. But this is not possible for NOAH, because it has no idea of why its critics do what they do. In addition, the correct solution requires abandoning a goal, a notion not even in NOAH's planning lexicon, as NOAH is not designed to handle interactions between goals originating from independent sources.

The purpose of this discussion is not to fault NOAH, for it indeed made many steps in the right direction. But, because it did not go far enough in considering the nature of interactions, its critics remain unstructured objects of only limited value. Raising the status of interactions forces the theory developed here to analyze critic-like functions in a more principled way and will provide answers to some of the more complex problems mentioned.

2.5 META-PLANNING PRINCIPLES

Another feature of our theory exemplified by story(2-1) has to do with the motivations of the planner itself. For example, we mentioned that the planner needs to know that, in general, it is a bad idea to create a plan that is wasteful, even if the plan achieves its intended goals. This is one of a number of guidelines for what constitutes a reasonable plan. Note that this guideline functions as a general principle in that it does not refer to particular facts about particular goals, but is applicable to virtually all planning situations. This is in contrast to the more usual knowledge about plans and goals, such as ''going to a store is a plan for getting possession of certain objects.'' This latter fact tells the planner what to do in a particular situation, whereas the former guideline tells the planner how to construct a plan in general.

Such guidelines are in fact goals of the planning process itself. Since they describe what the planner itself wants to accomplish, rather than particular plans and goals, we refer to this body of facts as *meta-planning* knowledge. At some level, the planner must embody this knowledge if it is to create sensible plans.

In the particular formulation of the theory of plans presented here, we formulate this *meta-planning* knowledge as explicit goals, plans, and so on. These ''meta-goals'' can then be submitted to the planning mechanism, which treats them just like any other goals. That is, the planner attempts to find a ''meta-plan'' for a meta-goal. The result of successful application of this plan will be the solution to the original planning problem.

The articulation of meta-planning knowledge is an important part of our theory of plans because it entails delineating the underlying principles of planning. In addition, the idea of presenting these principles as explicit plans and goals addresses the problems we mentioned earlier that arise from the shortcomings of critics. We discuss these principles of planning as well as the details and advantages of this particular formulation of meta-planning in Chapter 4.

2.6 PROJECTION AND REVISION

Another significant feature of our planning model is that it almost never produces a correct, complete plan in one pass. Rather, the current set of plans is continually revised in response to detected flaws and changes in the environment. In fact, since the planner is in principle detecting new goals all the time, the idea of a completed plan is only a relative notion.

In our model, the major mechanism through which problems with a plan are detected is called *projection*. As the planner formulates a plan, its execution is simulated in a hypothetical world model. Problems with proposed plans may be detected by examining these hypothetical worlds. Thus, if the planner in story (2-1) proposed the initial plan of making a separate trip to the store, he would simulate this plan and presumably find himself doing some extra traveling in his hypothetical future. This realization would then motivate the planner to try to find a better plan.

Projection not only enables the planner to find problems with its own plans, but it also enables it to determine that a situation merits having a new goal. For example, in order to sense an impending danger, the planner is required to project from the current state of affairs into a hypothetical world which it deems less desirable. Having made this projection, the planner can infer the goal of preventing the undesirable state of affairs from happening.

2.7 SHARED KNOWLEDGE

An important criterion in formulating our theory of plans is that it be usable for both understanding and for planning. Story (2-1) made use of some such facts about planning, such as "a way for getting milk is to buy some at a store." The constraint of using knowledge for two tasks means that the knowledge will have to be encoded highly declaratively. In a declarative format, a single form of the knowledge can be readily interpreted by a number of different processes; the format has other important advantages as well. This point is particularly important in motivating our structuring of meta-planning knowledge, a point discussed in more detail in Chapter 4.

2.8 SUMMARY

Having contrasted planning and understanding, we see them as two distinct but related tasks. Planning generally starts from a goal and proceeds toward a plan of action; understanding starts from perceived actions and proceeds toward hypothesized plans and goals. One desirable feature of our theory is a representation of plans that is useful for both tasks.

I am concerned here with the domain of commonplace activity in which most humans perform admirably. In this domain, planning and understanding are guided by large quantities of world knowledge. These processes probably do not require difficult computation, but the structure of the plans underlying them is more complex than that generally used in AI problem-solving programs.

In addition, the planner will have to infer its own goals and reason about the interaction between goals. It will have general principles of planning to guide it, as well as a mechanism for making hypotheses about the future. The knowledge needed for these features will be encoded so as to be accessible to understanding mechanisms as well.

3

Planning in Everyday Situations

3.1 INTRODUCTION

In this chapter, I present an overview of a model of planning. As was discussed in the previous chapters, this model is concerned with the routine sort of activities that occur in quite ordinary situations. The following story illustrates the areas of our concern.

(3-1)   *John was in a hurry to get to Las Vegas. However, he noticed that there were a lot of cops around, so he stuck to the speed limit.*

In story (3-1), the planner has the goal of being in Las Vegas soon. He realizes that a plan for this goal is to drive there at a high speed. However, the planner also realizes that this plan has a possible undesirable consequence, that is, it might result in the planner being ticketed. For this planner, avoiding this risk is apparently of greater importance than the original goal of getting to Las Vegas quickly. The planner therefore abandons the plan and settles for getting to his destination a bit more slowly.

The example points out a number of planning processes and knowledge structures that must exist in order to determine a course of action in simple situations. First, having established a goal, the planner must think of a plausible plan for it. Let us assume that the plan of driving fast is a ''canned plan'' for the goal of getting someplace quickly. That is, it is stored in memory as a plan applicable to this sort of goal and is retrievable as such. Thus we have the following requirements of a planner:

1. Plans are associated in memory with the goals to which they apply.
2. Plans that are associated with a particular goal can be retrieved from memory by specifying that goal.

Having located a plan applicable to his goal, the planner must now understand the implications of the plan. In particular, he must realize the interactions that this plan has with his other goals, implicit or explicit. For example, our planner trying to get to Las Vegas must realize that speeding may endanger his well-being or that of others, or that it might cause him to get a ticket. Of the effects this action might have, these side effects must be noted because they have some relevance to the planner's goal structure. Namely, getting hurt or being ticketed are generally undesirable states of affairs, and a planner who anticipates such occurrences should try to take some measures to prevent them from happening. Thus the following additional capabilities are essential for planning:

3. The planner can project plausible, hypothetical futures from its knowledge of the present world together with its own tentative plans.
4. Goals can be inferred based on the situation in which a planner finds itself.

Not only must our planner assess the significance of possible outgrowths of its current situation, but it must also understand the way in which these outgrowths relate to its plan. For example, the goal of avoiding getting a ticket has arisen in this situation as a direct consequence of our planner's efforts to fulfill another goal. An extremely naive planner, sensing the danger, might simply slow down without realizing that this would disrupt another task it had been trying to accomplish. This would lead to the failure of a goal without any consideration having been given to whether this is necessary or desirable. Or, if a planner notices that this task is in jeopardy, but is not capable of diagnosing an interaction, it might try to cure the problem by again planning to speed, then noticing the problem again, and so on, getting caught in an unproductive planning loop. Of course, we have no desire to construct such a naive planner, so we must supply our mechanism with the following features:

5. The planner must be capable of detecting the interactions between its goals.
6. These interactions must be taken into account in its subsequent planning processes.

''Taking interactions into account'' of course only suggests those processes of which a planner must actually be capable. Much attention will be paid to answering this question later on. However, at a minimum, a planner would need to be able to revise current plans to avoid a difficulty, or if this is not possible, choose among several nonideal alternative scenarios. For example, in story (1), the planner decides that getting to Las Vegas in a hurry is simply not worth the risk of getting a ticket and abandons his original goal altogether. So we have the following need:

7. In addition to generating and modifying plans for goals, the planner must be capable of evaluating alternative scenarios and of abandoning some goals in order to secure others.

In the rest of this chapter we present a model for planning motivated by the importance of the functions just outlined. In the next chapter we give a formulation of planning knowledge that will allow this control structure to apply to goal interactions, plan modification, decision problems, and other more complex maneuvers.

3.2 THE DESIGN OF A PLANNER FOR COMMON-SENSE REASONING

Most AI planning programs are given a single goal, for which they then attempt to formulate a plan. In contrast, our planner is to function in complex, changing environments. Thus its control structure has a more continuous flavor to it. This control structure is roughly the following: First, some state of affairs arises that causes the planner to realize that it should have a goal. For example, it might react to some internal state, such as hunger; to an external threat to some state it values or to some action that results in instilling it with an obligation. Once this goal is detected, a plan for it is proposed. Typically, if a standard plan for this goal is known to the planner, this plan will be suggested.

At this point, the planner must check to see if any of the new plans it has added interact with previous plans in a way relevant to the planner's goal structure. A detailed characterization of such interactions requires several chapters of this book. They include both negative interactions that preclude or reduce the possibility of a goal being fulfilled, as well as positive interactions that allow for the production of a more efficient overall plan.

In order to accommodate such interactions, the planner may try to revise its current plans. This process of checking for relevant interactions and proposing modifications to the current plan resembles the goal detection process of detecting relevant events and proposing goals. I will argue that this resemblance is not superficial and will present a formulation of planning knowledge that exploits the similarity.

In the process of proposing and modifying plans, additional goals could be encountered. For example, proposing a plan that entails a danger may cause the planner to have the goal of avoiding this pitfall; the revised planning structure may then include a measure to minimize risk, or it may abandon hope of fulfilling the original goal altogether. In addition, circumstances may change while planning is going on, resulting in the immediate obsolescence of an old goal or the introduction of yet another one. A desperate plan to obtain money to prevent foreclosure on a mortgage is not likely to be pursued after learning that one has inherited a fortune from a rich uncle. The introduction of an urgent crisis is likely to temporarily alter the planning structure for a leisurely afternoon.

Thus, rather than a simple, bounded algorithm, our planning mechanism is an iterative procedure which attempts to converge on an acceptable planning structure. After a period of plan proposing and editing, a *task network* of proposed actions results. This task network is a highly structured description of what the planner currently intends to do, containing intended actions, goals, and so on, along with numerous relations between these plan components.

Eventually the planner must begin executing these intended actions. The execution of an intended action is simply called an *action.* I will sometimes refer to intended actions as *plans,* when it is clear that the referent is a particular, executable task network component, and not a large, complex subcomponent of such a network. Execution will generally require the "expansion" of a plan—the filling in of details not considered when the plan was first proposed. At this level of detail, more interactions and problems might be detected, and a process similar to that described for initial plan formation will have to be undertaken. As the plan is executed, the task network must be updated to mark the current status of its various plans and goals.

3.3 THE COMPONENTS

To carry out this continuous planning procedure, I propose the following major components:

1. Goal Detector—This mechanism is responsible for determining that the planner has a goal. Essentially the Goal Detector notices situations (the mechanism for doing so to be described later) that have arisen that are relevant to the planner. A relevant situation may involve a change in the environment, the existence of another goal, or a problem in the current planning structure. Thus the Goal Detector must have access to the planner's likes, dislikes, and needs; to the state of the world and any changes that may befall it; and to the planner's own internal planning structures.

2. Plan Proposer—This component's task is to find stored plans relevant to current goals. It may dredge up stereotyped solutions, edit previously known plans to fit the current situation, or propose the novel use of a hitherto irrelevant action. The Plan Proposer is also responsible for expanding plans into component plans when necessary for further planning or execution, as this generally requires the proposal of a particular alternative.

3. Projector—The purpose of this component is to test plans by building hypothetical world models of what it would be like to execute these plans. Projecting the future requires considering other dynamics besides one's own plans, such as the probable actions of other planners or the course of natural events. Thus the Projector is actually a general-purpose simulator capable of predicting a possible future from a current set of beliefs. In planning, this ability is used to debug current plans by simulating a future that may contain undesirable elements, thus enabling the goal detector to form new goals aimed at improving this situation.

4. Executor—Once a stable plan structure has been achieved, the Executor tries to carry out the sequence of intended actions described in the task network. This may require expanding plans to a level of detail at which they can be directly executed and detecting interactions only noticeable at this level. The Executor must also monitor its progress by updating the task network to reflect changes in the status of various components.

The design of this planner is summarized in Fig. 3.1. As the various components just described are semi-autonomous, the arrows in the figure do not indicate strict flow of control, but rather, the input and output of the components. For example, the plan produced by the Plan Proposer is at one point input to the Projector; if it survives subsequent iterations, it will become input to the Executor.

3.3.1 Goal Detection in More Detail

The importance of the Goal Detector should be emphasized. As was mentioned previously, most planning systems do not worry about where their goals come from; high-level goals are generally handed to the planner in the form of a problem to be solved. However, a planning system needs to infer its own goals for a number of reasons. An autonomous planner needs to know when it should go into action; for example, it should be able to recognize that it is hungry or that its power supply is low and therefore what goal it should have. It should be able to take advantage of opportunities that present themselves, even if it doesn't have a particular goal in mind at the time. It should be able to protect itself from dangers in its environment, from other planners, or from consequences of its own plans.

The Goal Detector operates through the use of a mechanism called the *Noticer*. The Noticer is a general facility in charge of recognizing that something has occurred that is of interest to some part of the system. The Noticer monitors changes in the external environment and in the internal states of the system. When it detects the presence of something that it was previously instructed to monitor, it reports this occurrence to the source that originally told it to look for that event. The Noticer can be thought of as a collection of IF-ADDED demons (Charniak, 1972) whose only action is to report an event to some other mechanism.

Goals are detected by having descriptions of relevant situations asserted into the knowledge base of Noticer, along with orders to report the occurrence of an instance of one of these situations to the Goal Detector. For example, we can assert to the Noticer that when it gets hungry (i.e., when the value of some internal state reaches a certain point), the planner should have the goal of being not hungry (i.e., of changing this value); or that if someone is threatening to kill the planner, the planner should have the goal of protecting its life.

The Components of the Planner   **Figure 3.1**

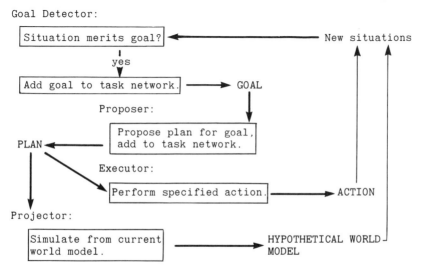

Schank and Abelson (1977) use the term "theme" to mean something that gives rise to a goal. Themes correspond, roughly, to a kind of labeling of the particular situation-goal pairs known to the Noticer. For example, one kind of theme discussed by Schank and Abelson is a role theme. This theme causes a planner to have a goal by virtue of his filling some role. Thus the professor grades his students' papers because his role as a professor requires him to do so. This sort of theme might be made functional in our planner by asserting a situation-goal pair of the form

Situation: X needs to be done and Planner has obligation to do X
Goal: Planner do X

When an event arises to which the planner is obliged to respond, this fact will inform it to do so, provided it has access to the knowledge associating the event with the appropriate obligation.

Note that the preceding situation-goal pair is a rather abstract fact, not specific to a particular domain. While the planner requires such general knowledge, all of the knowledge possessed in the Goal Detector is not necessarily of such an abstract character. Rather, arbitrarily specific, domain-dependent facts are assumed to abound. Often these facts will be more specific instances of facts also known to the system. The advantage of having available both general and specific versions of knowledge is that the specific information allows more familiar situations to be handled efficiently, whereas the general rules will still apply to those situations for which special purpose knowledge is not available.

For example, the planner possessing the preceding situation-goal pair might also possess the following situation-goal pair:

Situation: A student of Planner seeks to see Planner during office hours
Goal: Planner meet with student

The presence of this pair causes the planner to have the goal of meeting with the student upon learning of the student's need. The more general fact would have exactly the same effect, provided that the planner knew that it was obliged to meet with a student during office hours. However, the situation supplied to the Noticer by the more general fact explicitly requires determining if an obligation is involved, whereas the fact that seeing a student during office hours is an obligation does not play a causal role in determining the presence of the situation specified by the more specific version. Hence the more specific fact will allow for speedier goal detection in this particular situation. In effect, this specific fact is a kind of compiled version of the more general rule given a particular context.

In addition to speedier goal detection, knowing these specific facts has another advantage. There may be some knowledge useful in a particular situation, and the specialized situation descriptions that accompany the more specific facts, provide a useful means for organizing this knowledge. For example, if a standard plan is associated with a goal that occurs in a particular situation, it would be more efficient to associate this plan directly with that situation and select the plan at the same time the goal is detected. This would permit the planner to ''short-circuit'' part of the planning algorithm and suggest a plan immediately upon noticing a significant situation.

In the case of making a meeting with a student, a standard plan for the goal of making a meeting in this situation may be to arrange to meet in the planner's office. Rather than going through the additional step of detecting the particular goal and then trying to retrieve a normal plan for it, short-circuiting would make this plan immediately available upon recognizing the situation. This would be particularly important in cases in which timeliness is a factor. However, if the plan proposed in this manner interacted with other plans, the goal underlying the plan would still be available for more substantive reasoning. That is, short-circuiting does not otherwise counter the basic assumptions of the model except to make certain information available sooner than it might be otherwise.

The primary complication entailed by having specific facts subsumed by more general facts within the same system is that several facts will apply to a specific event. The result of a naive application of all pertinent knowledge would be a multiplicity of successively vaguer goals. This can lead to some ambiguity as to which goal to work on, since working on all of them simultaneously is redundant and possibly wasteful.

This problem is common to knowledge application situations in which hierarchies are present, which is precisely the structure to which our progressively more general situations correspond. The solution here is in fact based on a principle applicable in all such situations. This principle, termed the ''First Law of Knowledge Application,'' states:

Always apply the most specific pieces of knowledge available.

That is, when the choice exists between two otherwise equally applicable pieces of knowledge, employ the more specific of the two. In the case of a hierarchical set of situations in goal detection, the first law states that the planner should apply only the fact associated with the more specific situation. This is the correct solution here, because fulfilling the most specific goal logically entails fulfilling the more general ones as well.

To implement this constraint within our planner, associations can be maintained from a specific fact to a more general fact from which it arises. In addition, these facts can be indexed in the Noticer so that the more specific fact will be found before the more general one in those situations in which they both apply. Having noticed the situation, the Noticer can mark the situations above it in a hierarchy and ignore them in its search for additional applicable knowledge.

The tension between general and specific knowledge found in goal detection will arise repeatedly in other processes in both planning and understanding. Much of what has been said will also apply to these situations. However, in most of the discussion that follows, I emphasize the more general knowledge over the more particular facts that may also be present and ignore the kind of interactions described previously. The primary reason for this is that the more general facts are basic to an understanding of a particular phenomena, and thereby to the basic operation of the processes that deal with them. By contrast, the more particular facts simply improve a system's performance, but do not shed any light on a theoretically interesting structure.

3.3.2 The Proposer and the Projector

The Proposer begins by suggesting the most specific plan it knows of that is applicable to the goal. If this plan is rejected or fails, the Proposer proposes successively more general and "creative" solutions. Once the Proposer has suggested a plan, the Projector starts computing what will happen to the world as the plan is executed. The difficult problems in conducting a simulation involve reasoning about "possible world" situations which are not amenable to standard temporal logic (McCarthy and Hayes, 1969). Rather than employ a logic for possible worlds (cf. Moore, 1980), this issue is finessed here by defining hypothetical states in terms of what the planner thinks of in the course of plan construction. In other words, the solution is to let the system assert the changes that would be made into a hypothetical data base, in the meantime letting the Goal Detector have access to these states. Thus, if the plan being simulated would result in the planner dying, say, this would constitute a hypothetical, undesirable state, which might trigger the addition of the goal of revising the plan to prevent this impending disaster.

Actually the function of the Projector is somewhat more pervasive than has so far been described. The Projector must be capable of projecting current events into future possibilities based both on the intentions of the planner and on its analysis of those events themselves. For example, if the planner sees a boulder rolling down the mountain, the Projector's job is to project the future path that the boulder will traverse. If the projected path crosses that of the planner, for example, a preservation goal should be detected. Thus the Projector is a quite powerful and general device that is capable of predicting plausible futures.

3.4 PANDORA

At Berkeley, we have implemented a program called PANDORA (Plan Analysis with Dynamic Organization, Revision, and Application) that uses this model to propose plans, simulate probable futures, and detect goals. However, the model, as described thus far, does not possess the capability to deal with the more complex aspects of planning that we initially claimed were central to processing complex situations. For example, we showed how goal detection and projection could be used to spot a bug in a plan, such as the planner inadvertently killing itself. But we have not indicated how the planner could fix this problem with the apparatus provided. In the next chapter, we offer a way of formulating knowledge about such interactions so that our planner can be used to function in circumstances involving these complexities.

4

Meta-Planning

4.1 INTRODUCTION

The planner sketched out in the previous chapter, if supplied with the appropriate knowledge, is able to propose straightforward plans for some goals and to simulate the effect of carrying out these plans. However, I have not specified the manner in which this planner could deal with goal interactions and with plan debugging and modification. These problems are now addressed.

First, consider a goal interaction such as the following:

(4- 1)   John wanted to go out with Mary, but he was afraid his wife would find out.

Here John has the goal of dating Mary and also the conflicting goal of preventing his wife from learning this intention. Several possible courses of action are open to him. He can ask Mary out and risk his wife's wrath. He can forego dating Mary so as not to risk upsetting his wife. Or he can make a date with Mary, taking care to plan this date in such a manner so that his wife will not suspect his activities.

Unfortunately our planner could not yet choose any of these options. The first two require abandoning one goal in favor of another, and so far we have not postulated any mechanism for purposefully abandoning a goal. The third alternative cannot be generated either, as it requires producing a plan taking into account two goals at once, and we have no mechanism for such a process.

Not only do we not have the mechanisms for generating these plans, but there is nothing in the nature of the planning mechanism we have described that even explains why they are reasonable plans. For example, giving up dating Mary because it is viewed as a risk to John's marriage is a reasonable plan because it is reasonable to give up one goal for a more important goal. However, so far the model has only treated goals in isolation. Thus the planner has no motivation to consider abandoning a goal, as this requires reasoning about a whole collection of goals at once.

A planner may wish to abandon an individual goal because the planner itself has a set of overriding purposes. An example of one such purpose is to try to achieve the goals that are valued the most. This broad purpose would be useful as it would inform the planner about how to choose in the case of a dilemma such as the one in which John finds himself.

I refer to this class of facts as *meta-planning* knowledge. This term refers to knowledge about the planning process itself. For example, the fact that a planner should abandon one goal in order to fulfill another, less important goal is a meta-planning fact. This is because this fact refers not to how some particular goal should be fulfilled, but to how the planner should behave with respect to goals in general.

4.2 THE FORMULATION OF META-PLANNING KNOWLEDGE

As the example in the preceding section indicates, meta-planning knowledge is highly intentional in nature. In effect, it constitutes the goals of the planning mechanism. The formulation of this knowledge offered here takes this analogy to ordinary goals rather literally. That is, knowledge about how to plan is expressed in terms of a set of goals for the planning process (called *meta-goals*) and a set of plans to achieve them (*meta-plans*). As we will see, the point of expressing this knowledge in terms of goals and plans is that the same planning mechanism that is used to produce a plan for simple situations can operate in the more complex domain of goal interactions.

For example, in story (4-1) a meta-goal involved is to resolve the conflict between the two "ordinary" goals stated in the text. One meta-plan for this goal is to replan the plan for the first goal so as not to cause a conflict with the second. In this particular case, this might mean executing the plan for the first in a discreet manner to avoid detection by John's wife.

Once we express this knowledge in terms of meta-goals and meta-plans, we need to specify the circumstances under which the planner will have such goals. Following the analogy to ordinary goals, we need to describe those situations, labeled *meta-themes*, under which the planner should possess particular meta-goals. For example, one such meta-theme would be **ACHIEVE AS MANY GOALS AS POSSIBLE**. This theme would cause the planner to have the meta-goal of resolving a goal conflict whenever a goal conflict situation came into being.

By expressing knowledge about goal conflict and other interactions in the form of explicit meta-planning entities, we can derive considerable power from the planning mechanism described in the previous chapter. For example, because a goal conflict is a situation in which a meta-goal (of resolving a goal conflict) should be detected, the goal detection mechanism proposed in Chapter 3 can be used to detect this meta-goal when a goal conflict arises. Then the plan-proposing mechanism can suggest meta-plans for this goal, the successful execution of which will result in a better plan for the original goals. Thus tasks such as the detection of goal conflicts and revising previous plans can be handled by the machinery already proposed, provided that we can formulate meta-planning knowledge in a suitable manner.

4.3 KINDS OF META-ENTITIES

The specific meta-goals and meta-plans that the model is to contain are of course of great importance to us here. However, most of these entities refer to kinds of goal interactions that have yet to be described. I will therefore develop the details of particular meta-plans and meta-goals in the subsequent chapters as I describe how to process situations involving each goal relationship.

This section gives an overview of meta-themes and an example of how these would actually function in processing complex situations. In the example, a great number of meta-planning entities will be referred to, although no organization or justification of these entities is given. This is reserved for later chapters; the example is meant only to give the flavor of planning using meta-planning.

All the meta-planning entities I have encountered can be organized under four main principles, or meta-themes, which give rise to various meta-goals as a function of the situation. These meta-themes are:

1. DON'T WASTE RESOURCES
2. ACHIEVE AS MANY GOALS AS POSSIBLE
3. MAXIMIZE THE VALUE OF THE GOALS ACHIEVED
4. AVOID IMPOSSIBLE GOALS

For example, the meta-theme **ACHIEVE AS MANY GOALS AS POSSIBLE** is responsible for detecting goal conflicts. That is, if the planner intends to perform a set of actions that will negatively interact with one another, this meta-theme causes the planner to have the goal of resolving the conflict. If this meta-goal fails, i.e., the planner could not find a way to resolve the conflict, the meta-theme **MAXIMIZE THE VALUE OF THE GOALS ACHIEVED** springs into action. This meta-theme sets up the goal of arriving at a scenario in which the less valuable goals are abandoned in order to fulfill the most valuable ones.

The meta-theme **DON'T WASTE RESOURCES** embodies the desire to produce efficient plans. For example, in a situation involving two goals each of which has a plan requiring the same precondition, this meta-theme would be responsible for generating a meta-goal of scheduling the two plans so that the precondition need be fulfilled only once. Thus a planner who wanted two items available at the same store would use this meta-theme to help formulate a plan containing only one trip to this store and followed by purchasing both items, as opposed to making two separate trips.

AVOID IMPOSSIBLE GOALS is needed to prevent proposing goals for which no plans are possible. Preventing circular planning structures is the purview of this meta-theme, for example. The meta-theme will also instruct the planner to abandon a goal that seems hopeless.

No doubt there are other ways to carve up the knowledge organized by these principles. For example, all these principles could be merged into one **MAXIMIZE OVERALL OUTCOME** principle. One need only consider preserving a resource as a goal, note that fulfilling all one's goals will always maximize the value of those achieved, and recognize that entertaining an impossible goal will at best waste some planning resources.

Although having one **MAXIMIZE OVERALL OUTCOME** principle is harmonious with the approach taken here, I have resisted this consolidation for two reasons. First, I want to maintain the intuitive difference I see between the four categories listed. For example, I believe that there is a real psychological difference between a goal like actively trying to preserve one's money, and the notion of not squandering it in the execution of some buying plan. Second, the categories are useful in organizing the particular meta-goals and meta-plans that the system requires in any event. For example, trying to resolve a conflict and abandoning a goal when such a resolution cannot be found are two quite different strategies that are appropriate in different situations. That is, the planner needs to know that abandoning a goal should be done only when all one's goals cannot be fulfilled. This is essentially the distinction between **ACHIEVE AS MANY GOALS AS POSSIBLE** and **MAXIMIZE THE VALUE OF THE GOALS ACHIEVED**. Thus the system requires something equivalent to this distinction, regardless of whether the distinction is recognized in terms of meta-themes or in terms of some less prominent distinction.

Actually these terms serve more as labels than as anything else. The planner uses this knowledge by proposing meta-goals in response to detecting certain situations. Thus the content of the model is largely concerned with the descriptions of the particular situations and corresponding meta-goals that the planner must have to function. As the preceding discussion suggests, this content would probably remain invariant if a somewhat different organization were imposed upon it. The particular meta-themes given here serve to organize this knowledge for exposition more than they constrain the causal structure of the planner itself.

4.4   AN EXAMPLE

The following example illustrates the use of meta-planning entities in the planning process. Suppose a planner were given the task of fetching a newspaper from outside during a rain storm. The planner will first consider the "normal" plan for a task if one is known. The normal plan for getting the newspaper is walking outside and carrying it back in, which in this case would cause the planner to get its clothes wet. Proposing this plan would therefore cause the Goal Detector to determine that the ''Don't Violate Desirable States'' theme should be invoked, and thereby to create a Preserve-Endangered-State(Clothes be dry) goal.

Since this preservation goal came into existence as the result of some intended action by the planner itself, a conflict exists between this goal and the goal from which the other action originated. Since a goal conflict threatens the fulfillment of a goal, the Goal Detector acts once again. This time the meta-theme **ACHIEVE AS MANY GOALS AS POSSIBLE** causes the meta-goal *RESOLVE-GOAL-CONFLICT(G1, P1)* to come into existence, where G1 is the goal of having the newspaper and P1 the goal of preserving the dryness of the planner's clothing. The state of planning at this point is diagrammed in Fig. 4.1.

Now a plan for this meta-goal is sought. Since a meta-goal is treated just like an ordinary goal by the planner, normal plans for resolving the conflict are sought first. That is, we apply the *USE-NORMAL-PLAN* metal-plan, which looks for a plan specifically designed to resolve this particular kind of goal conflict. One such stored plan for this situation is to wear a raincoat while performing the plan for goal G1. Suppose the planner proposed this plan, which spawns the subgoal of acquiring a raincoat. If a raincoat were readily available, the plan for resolving the goal conflict succeeds and the plan for G1 can be executed.

On the other hand, the subgoal of obtaining a raincoat might spawn a plan that involves going outside to buy one if one is not readily available. As this is a circular subgoal, the **AVOID IMPOSSIBLE GOALS** meta-theme causes the Goal Detector to initiate a *RESOLVE-CIRCULAR-GOALS(G1, S1)* meta-goal, where S1 is the circular subgoal just created. A meta-plan applicable here is *REPLAN*, which tries to choose another plan that does not spawn subgoal S1. Suppose that this fails, and no other canned plan for achieving the *RESOLVE-GOAL-CON-FLICT(G1, P1)* meta-goal can be found. Since a meta-goal is treated just like any

Task Network after Detection of the Conflict   **Figure 4.1**

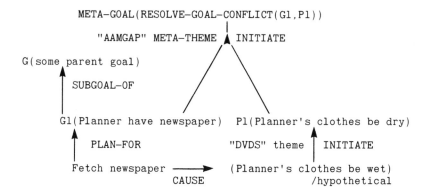

other goal, the planner might try to create a more novel plan here. The more novel plans for goal conflict resolution are ***TRY-ALTERNATE-PLAN*** and ***CHANGE-CIRCUMSTANCES***. For example, the planner might try the alternative plan of getting his dog to fetch the paper, as this plan does not involve the planner getting wet. Or the planner might try to alter the circumstances that enable an intended action to have its undesirable effect. For example, the planner might try interposing some object in between himself and the rain, like an old newspaper, or simply wait for the rain to stop. Both waiting and actively changing a circumstance are general strategies applied to this particular situation.

Suppose that such plans are not generated or are rejected for other reasons. Then the planner has failed to fulfill its ***RESOLVE-GOAL-CONFLICT*** goal. The existence of an unresolvable goal conflict indicates that some goal is about to fail, and the Goal Detector is called into play again, allowing the **MAXIMIZE THE VALUE OF THE GOALS ACHIEVED** meta-theme to create a CHOOSE-MOST-VALUABLE-SCENARIO(G1, P1) meta-goal. The plan for this goal is SIMULATE-AND-SELECT. This meta-plan works by invoking the subgoal CREATE-ALTERNATIVE-SCENARIOS(G1, P1), evaluating each proposed scenario and then adopting the scenario that is deemed most attractive. The situation at this point is as shown in Fig. 4.2

In this case, ***CREATE-ALTERNATIVE-SCENARIOS*** has a relatively straightforward task, as there are only two scenarios: Abandoning G1, or abandoning P1. (Actually, ***CREATE-ALTERNATIVE-SCENARIOS*** is more complex, as it also has the possibility of proposing "partial goal achievement" scenarios. For example, it might suggest only partially achieving P1, that is, achieving "Keep clothes as dry as possible," in which case a suitable plan might be to run out to get the paper.) Now the planner has to make a judgment on the relative value of the goals involved. To make this evaluation, we assume that the planner is able to attach some sort of value on each of its goals, say, a value between 0 (don't care) and 10 (life or death). The value of each scenario is defined as the sum of the value of its individual goals. If "not getting my best suit wet" is a 5 and "having the paper" is a 3, the two scenarios have a relative value of 5 and 3, so P1 is selected over G1. In this case, the planner stays inside and does without his paper.

Scenarios involving partial goal achievement are handled the same way. For example, if getting one's clothes just a trifle wet is a 2, then that scenario is valued as a 7 (since one ends up with the paper as well), and would be chosen over either of the two more polarized versions. (In general, goal abandonment is a strategy of last resort. A planner is much more likely to try to replan away the problem or to use partial goal achievement as a strategy. For example, a planner is likely to listen to the news on the radio, wait for the rain to stop, try to get someone else to bring in the paper, change to less valuable clothing, use something instead of a raincoat, and so on, instead of abandoning the goal altogether.)

4.5   META-PLANNING, CONSTRAINTS, AND CRITICS

In addition to the power meta-planning lends to the planning mechanism just outlined, it entails a number of other advantages. Some of the major benefits of this formulation are now described.

4.5.1   More General Resolution of Traditional Planning Problems

Meta-planning knowledge generally embodies a set of strategies for complicated plan interactions. By formulating this knowledge in terms of goals and plans, the same planning architecture that already exists for simpler planning can be used to implement more complicated planning involving multiple goals, and so on. For example, in order to debug a problematic plan, such as one containing a goal conflict, a planner may first try to resolve the problem by applying canned meta-plans. If these fail, the planner may try to construct progressively more novel plans. This is precisely the strategy we have assumed the planner would use to select a suitable plan for an ordinary goal.

Task Network After Failure to Resolve the Conflict   **Figure 4.2**

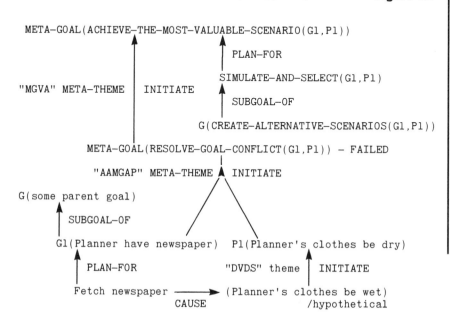

In contrast, more traditional planners usually treat problems such as goal conflicts by special purpose means—by the introduction of critics, for example (Sussman, 1975; Sacerdoti, 1977). Critics are essentially routines that procedurally embody knowledge about how to treat particular kinds of defects in plans. Thus employing a critic is equivalent to having the general problem solver consult an expert when it gets into trouble.

The meta-planning approach separates the formulation of the problem from its detection and solution. Activating a meta-goal corresponds to detecting a problem, the meta-goal itself to the formulation of the problem, and finding an appropriate meta-plan to creating a solution. The advantage of this approach is that it allows the general problem solver to solve planning problems by calling a general problem solver itself. Thus all the power of such a system can be focused on planning problems, rather than just relying on expert tactics.

Of course, all the specific knowledge usually embodied in a critic is still available in the meta-planning approach, generally in the form of canned meta-plans. But the meta-planning model allows this knowledge to interact with all other knowledge as it now takes part in general reasoning processes.

Another planning mechanism employed by traditional planners involves the use of constraints, or states whose violation is explicitly prohibited (Stefik, 1980). Generally, if a constraint is violated, a plan is rejected and it is left to the plan generator to propose a new plan. In our model, proposing to use a plan that violates a particular condition would cause the creation of a meta-goal that represents this problem. The existence of this meta-goal would cause the planner to try to solve this particular problem, rather than just return control to the plan generator. This meta-planning approach does not embody the asymmetry between constraints and goals in more traditional systems: constraints can only block plans, but cannot themselves propose new ones.*

McDermott's notion of a *policy*, or a secondary task, comes closest to the notion of meta-planning I propose here (McDermott, 1977). A policy is essentially an explicitly represented constraint. Like meta-goals, policies have the advantage that they may easily enter into general computations. The primary differences between a policy and a meta-goal are that meta-goals are meant to be more general and include goals that are not necessarily constraints per se; meta-goals refer only to facts about planning as their domain, whereas policies (and constraints in general) may include domain-specific information; policies often entail the creation of pseudo-tasks, whereas meta-goals have meta-plans that deviate less from the structure of normal plans.

4.5.2 Representational Advantages

The meta-planning model also provides more flexibility when no ideal solution to a problem can be found. Since a meta-goal represents the formulation of a problem,

---

*Herb Simon pointed out this asymmetry to me.

the existence of the problem may be dealt with beyond its being solved. For example, the problem solver may simply decide to accept a flawed plan if the violation is viewed as not being too important, or decide to abandon one of the goals that it cannot satisfy. By separating solving the problem from formulating the problem, the problem may be accessed as opposed to treated, an option that most other problem-solving models do not allow.

4.5.3   Using Meta-Planning for Both Planning and Understanding

As meta-goals and meta-plans are declarative structures, they may be used to understand situations as well as to plan in them. An understander with access to this knowledge would be able to interpret someone's action as an attempt to resolve a goal conflict, for example. The ability to use meta-planning knowledge for understanding is an advantage not shared by planning programs that have this knowledge embedded procedurally, since procedural embedding generally makes that knowledge less amenable to uses other than that at which the code was explicitly targeted. In the next chapter, we will describe more fully the process of understanding and the role that meta-planning plays in it.

4.6   A SIMPLE PANDORA EXAMPLE

This model of planning and meta-planning is used by PANDORA to reason its way through a variety of situations. Consider the following example of PANDORA operating in an everyday domain. Since PANDORA's reasoning is done by the manipulation of representations rather than linguistic utterances, the example is somewhat cryptic. The comments are supplied to alleviate this problem. A more detailed description of PANDORA and the representations it uses, along with additional, more complex examples, are found in the final chapters.

```
INITIAL STATE:
(TimeOfDay (Time Morning))
;it is morning
(Weather (Object (Outside)) (Condition Raining))
;It is raining
PLAN PRODUCED:
((PutOn (Actor (Ego)) (Object (Raincoat)))
;Put on a raincoat
(Ptrans (Actor (Ego)) (Object (Ego)) (To (Outside)))
;Go outside
(Grasp (Actor (Ego)) (Object (Newspaper)))
;Pick up the newspaper
(Ptrans (Actor (Ego)) (Object (Ego)) (To (Inside)))
;Go Inside
(Read (Actor Ego) (Object (Newspaper)))
```

In creating this plan, PANDORA first detects its normal morning goal of finding out what is happening in the world. Then the normal plan for this goal is proposed, namely, walking outside, picking up the paper, bringing it back in, and reading it. However, when the scenario that includes this plan is projected into the future, the Noticer determines that PANDORA will get wet and informs the Goal Detector, which infers the goal of preserving dryness. Next, the Goal Detector together with the Noticer find the resulting goal conflict between going outside and staying dry. The Plan Proposer proposes a meta-plan for this goal, in this case, *USE-NORMAL-PLAN*. The execution of this meta-plan results in retrieving a stored normal plan for this situation, namely, wearing a raincoat while executing the original plan. Thus PANDORA's final plan contains this measure, which would not normally be included in PANDORA's morning routine.

PANDORA has also been applied to the domain of using the UNIX* operating system. In this domain, PANDORA serves as the problem-solving component of the UC (UNIX Consultant) natural language interface to UNIX. The discussion of PANDORA in Chapter 12 includes examples from this domain as well.

4.7 RELATION TO OTHER WORK

The use of the term *meta-knowledge* to describe the knowledge a system possesses about its own knowledge or capabilities has become common in AI (e.g., see Davis and Buchanan, 1977, and Barr, 1977). For the most part, this usage refers to a quite different concept from that denoted by the term *meta-planning* used here. Meta-knowledge generally refers to any fact that directly references another fact, whereas I use the term meta-planning to refer to facts about planning. There are two significant consequences of this distinction.

First, meta-knowledge is a more general concept, including any fact that describes another fact. For example, the fact that some ordinary fact is used infrequently would be a piece of meta-knowledge. However, such a fact would have no special status in the knowledge base of the planner described here.

Second, meta-knowledge is generally construed to allow domain-specific meta-facts, i.e., facts about facts about particular domains. For example, the fact that some particular fact is used infrequently is in effect a fact about a particular domain and will not be useful in tasks ouside that domain. By contrast, the intent of meta-planning knowledge is for it to refer only to the planning process and thereby to be independent of and hence applicable to any domain in which the planner is operating.

The two usages overlap substantially, however, in that a prime use of meta-knowledge is in the selection of knowledge applicable to a given task (Davis, 1977). In Davis's system, TEIRESIAS, ordinary knowledge is expressed in rules,

---

*UNIX is a trademark of Bell Laboratories

and knowledge about how to use this knowledge is expressed in meta-rules. For example, Davis and Buchanan (1977) give the following instance of a meta-rule applicable to an investment counseling scenario:

If   1. you are attempting to determine the best stock to invest in,
*   2. the client's tax status is non-profit,*
*   3. there are rules which mention in their premise the income-tax bracket of the client,*
then   it is very likely (.9) that each of these rules is not going to be useful.

The rule is a meta-rule in that it makes a predication about other rules. It is related to meta-planning in that the fact would be used in an expert system to instruct the system, not to examine the rules in question given the particular situation referred to in the premise of the meta-rule.

Note that this particular meta-rule is quite domain specific, i.e., it is strictly a fact about knowledge about investing. It is in this respect that the difference between meta-knowledge and meta-planning is most clearly revealed. In the formulation of meta-planning knowledge advocated here, facts about how to use facts, in order to be part of meta-planning knowledge, would not be able to refer to domain-specific facts at all. For example, to select among competing alternatives, the planner might apply a meta-plan designed to make such a choice. Such a meta-plan might require recourse to particular facts about the plans available. For example, without anything else to go on, the meta-plan might select the most frequently successful plan. This would require storing the frequency of success of an operator, technically a piece of meta-knowledge. But this fact would be stored in the planner's knowledge base along with ordinary facts.

In effect, the content of this meta-plan would be the quite general idea of using the plan promising the greatest chance of success. Since the particular facts about which plans are successful in which situations are just data to this meta-plan, the meta-plan is not restricted to operate in any particular domain. Instead, it need only be supplied with knowledge about the relative promise of plans in a given domain to function in that domain.

An idea more similar to the notion of meta-planning proposed here, and bearing the same name, has been proposed independently by Stefik (1980). Stefik uses meta-planning to address control issues that arise in the design of problem-solving systems. For the design of the MOLGEN expert system, he proposes a multiple-layered system in which each layer is essentially another problem solver dedicated to the problems that arise on the previous layer. This control structure is used to replace the single, complex interpreter one would find in a nonlayered, agenda-based system.

Stefik's notion of meta-planning addresses some of the same issues I address here, but our solutions are formulated in somewhat different ways. In particular, Stefik does not formulate his meta-level problem solvers in terms of explicit meta-goals; instead, specific strategies are employed on each level. MOLGEN represents its problem-level goals and constraints explicitly, but it does not have explicit representations of meta-level goals or of meta-constraints (i.e., constraints involved in the reasoning process itself).

While MOLGEN does not embody explicit meta-goals, they would seem to be compatible with the nature of that system. Indeed, what differences there are in our respective formulations are more probably the result of the differences in the task domain than of incompatible theoretical views. However, at least one feature of Stefik's formulation is explicitly resisted in my analysis—the division of MOLGEN into a multiple-level problem solver. The multiple-level approach assumes that there is little in common about the structure of problem solving on each layer, and that therefore the best solution is to have a separate problem solver for each level.

The approach taken here makes exactly the opposite assumption. Namely, that planning and meta-planning are essentially the same sort of activity; only different goals and plans are specified in each case. The relative efficiency and psychological accuracy that might be attributed in principle to either design will probably take considerable time and experimental effort to discern.

Hayes-Roth and Hayes-Roth (1979) use the term meta-planning to refer to decisions about the planning process. Although my use of the term is similar to theirs, they include all types of planning decisions under this name, and their meta-planning knowledge is not formulated in terms of explicit meta-planning entities. I use the term to refer only to a subset of this knowledge, and only when that knowledge is expressed in terms of explicit meta-goals and meta-plans.

4.8 SUMMARY

In sum, meta-planning allows problems faced by the planner to be formulated as goals and then given to the planner to solve in a general fashion. Because of the explicit, declarative nature of this formulation, the approach appears to have a number of advantages over the more usual approaches used to handle interaction between plan components. In particular, the declarative representation should facilitate the use of the same knowledge in the understanding process as well.

We now turn to the problem of understanding. First, we examine this process in general and suggest a model which emphasizes the role played by planning knowledge. Having done so, we further examine the formulation of planning strategies using meta-planning with respect to the utility of this formulation in understanding situations involving goal interactions.

5

Explanation-Driven Understanding

5.1 INTRODUCTION

Understanding a text involves finding the implicit connections between sentences. Thus much of the work in this area is concerned with the problem of inference generation (Charniak, 1972; Riegen, 1975a; Schank and Rieger, 1974; Joshi and Rosenschein, 1976). In particular, the problem of representing knowledge needed for understanding has dominated this work, and involves the notions of scripts and plans (Schank and Abelson, 1977), schemata (Rumelhart, 1976) and frames (Minsky, 1974). Several story understanding programs have been based on such formalisms. For example, Cullingford's SAM system (Cullinford, 1978) uses scripts to understand a variety of stereotyped situations; Charniak's Ms. Malaprop program (Charniak, 1978) uses frame-based representations toward a similar end.

The basic idea behind most of these approaches is illustrated by the following story, which is used by (Schank and Abelson, 1977) to demonstrate their script idea:

(5- 1) John went to a restaurant. The hostess seated John. The hostess gave John a menu. John ordered a lobster. He was served quickly. He left a large tip. He left the restaurant.

The point of this example is to demonstrate that knowledge about what typically goes on at a restaurant is needed to infer implicit events, such as John's eating the lobster. The notion of a script is introduced as a way to organize such knowledge.

As was pointed out by their inventors at the time of their inception, rigid knowledge structures such as scripts are inadequate for much of the inference processing necessary to establish the coherence of many texts. Script-like knowledge structures reflect the repeated experience of specific situations and are directly useful for comprehending these situations. However, they are less clearly useful for processing situations that do not conform entirely to stereotypes. Furthermore, as there is little point in expressing events that strictly conform to a known stereotype, most of the actual texts we might encounter will refer to situations for which such rigid knowledge structures are not well suited.

5.1.1 Explanation-Driven Understanding

Understanding a situation that is not necessarily stereotypical requires reasoning mechanisms other than those that script-based processing can provide. In particular, script-based understanding tends to be rather inflexible. If an event occurs that is not in the script being used to understand a text, it cannot be handled by a script-based mechanism. For example, consider the following story:

(5- 2) *John wanted to impress Mary. He asked Fred if he could borrow his Mercedes for the evening.*

It is unlikely that most understanders process this example using a script. To claim as much would amount to saying that whenever a reader hears that someone wants to impress a date, the reader then expects to hear of the person asking a friend to loan him a fancy car. A script that includes all such alternatives is an impossibility in any case, since we could always create new variations not already in the package.

Even if it were possible to include an infinitude of variation within a script, doing so would defeat the purpose behind the script concept. Scripts are supposed to constrain the inference process by specifying events that are usually found in mundane sequences. Clearly, scripts would not be mundane or inference-constraining if they explicitly delineate all possible alternatives.

Although script processing is inherently limited to understanding those event sequences that conform to a rigid structure, human readers seem to have no trouble connecting up the events in texts like story (5-2). Since people can easily understand texts with some novel variation in them, a more general theory of text coherence is needed to describe the processing of these situations. I call the general process of finding the connection between events in a text *explanation-driven understanding*. That is, much of the processing that a reader needs to do to understand a text revolves around the task of finding explanations for the events of the text. Since stories are generally about people, explanations usually take on an intentional flavor. The reader must find explanations for people's behavior, and these explanations will be stated in terms of a person's plans and goals.

For example, in story (5-2), John's asking Fred to loan him a car is explained by inferring that this action is part of a plan for a goal of getting possession of a vehicle. This goal is explained by inferring that it is instrumental to John's plan of picking up his date in an expensive car. This plan is explained in turn by John's desire to impress his date, which is explicitly stated in the story.

Thus a reader of story (5-2) must compute a series of explanatory inferences in order to understand John's action. Each of these inferences explains some element of John's behavior—why he has a goal, why he chooses a plan, or why he performs an action. In each case, the type of explanation that can be found is a function of the type of element that is to be explained. That is, an explanation is intuitively construed as a reasonable plan for a goal. Thus a particular element will be explained by its role in a hypothesized task network. Since different types of elements can participate only in certain relations to certain classes of other elements of a plan, different types of elements will require different types of explanations. In sum, permissible classes of explanation will mirror the permission structures allowable in a task network.

For example, consider the status of an action vis-à-vis a plan. An action relates rationally to a plan structure only if it is thought to constitute an attempt to execute a piece of a plan. Thus an action can be explained by finding it to be an instantiation of a plan its actor is pursuing. According to this rule, in story (5-2), John's asking action would be explained by hypothesizing that it instantiates a step of John's plan to borrow Bill's car.

Similarly, a plan, or intended action, can appear in a larger plan structure only as a means to fulfill a goal. Thus a plan can be explained by determining that it is applicable to some goal of its planner. In story (5-2), this would mean that John's plan to borrow a car must be explained by some goal, namely, that goal of wanting to possess a car for some time period.

Unlike plans and actions, goals can occur in two places in a simple plan structure. They can be given rise to by themes, or they can occur as subgoals, aimed at fulfilling a precondition of another piece of the plan. Therefore, a goal can be explained if it is found to be instrumental to some plan, or if a theme can be found that gives rise to the goal. In story (5-2), John's goal of possessing the car could be explained by the existence of possession as a precondition for John's plan of using the car. On the other hand, John's ultimate goal, which might have been to succeed with Mary in some manner, might be explained by determining that it arose from a basic theme of being accepted by the opposite sex.

The types of intentional explanations derived from the structure of simple plans are summarized in Table 5.1.

5.1.2 Inferring Explanations in Context

Table 5.1 describes the constituents of an explanation. But it does not describe how an explanation is constructed for a sentence in a text. The major consideration that

Types of Intentional Explanations — Table 5.1

Item to Explain	Explanation
Action	Plan that the action instantiates
Plan	Goal at which the plan is directed
Goal	Theme that gives rise to the goal, or plan to which the goal is instrumental

this theory must take into account is how the context of a text can influence the particular explanation that is constructed without making the inference process too rigid to accommodate reasonable variations. For example, suppose a reader were given the following stories.

(5- 3) A bum on the street came over to John. He told John he wanted some money.
(5- 4) A man came over to John and pulled out a gun. He told John he wanted some money.
(5- 5) John's son came over to John. He told John he wanted some money.

In these cases, the second sentence of each text has a different interpretation, even though the sentences are the same. The interpretations are different because they are influenced by the context set up by the first sentence. However, the context does not totally determine the interpretation, as it would in a script-governed situation. For example, in story (5-5), John's son coming over to him does not determine that his son would ask him for something, although it does bias the subsequent processing. The problem is how to allow the context to influence the interpretation while still allowing enough latitude to explain unexpected events.

A general scheme by which plausible, context-sensitive explanations can be inferred is essentially a "shortest path" algorithm that finds a connection between the new input and a piece of the story's current representation in memory. That is, when an explanation is needed for some element in a text (i.e., an action, a plan, or a goal), the items already known to the reader are checked first to see if any of them could constitute an explanation. This check is directed by the syntax of the allowable explanations given earlier and is done against a knowledge base of semantically acceptable relations. If a semantically acceptable connection between the input and a known item can be found, this item is construed to be the explanation for the input.

If no such item is currently in the reader's story representation, the reader consults its general world knowledge, without regard to the context of the story, to find explanatory relationships in which the input is known to participate. Again, this consultation is directed by the structure of syntactically allowable explanation forms and is made against a knowledge base of semantically sensible relations. However, since this step is not constrained to find a relation to some item already in the representation, a new item may be retrieved from memory as a potential explanation. If so, the reader hypothesizes this item as the explanation for the input.

Since this new item is not otherwise related to the story representation, the reader sets out to determine such a relation by finding an explanation for the item hypothesized as the explanation for the original input. This is done by reentering the process just described with the new item as an input.

The entire process is iterated until either an explanation has been constructed that relates the input to a previous part of the story, or suitable candidates for explanations can no longer be found. During this process, several explanatory inferences could be made about a particular input. In this case, all these rival explanations are carried along, and explanations for each of them are sought breath-first. The first "explanation chain" that connects up to a known story event is maintained, and the others are discarded. If more than one chain of the same length is found, the input has an ambiguous explanation, which is assumed not to be the case in most noncontrived stories. In the case of the beginning of an episode, the process allows the explanation to terminate by inferring a theme, which need not connect up to previous parts of the story, as there may be none. However, after this initial phase, nonconnecting thematic explanations will be deferred in favor of those that connect to a previous part of the story representation.

For example, if the input to be explained is an action, the story representation is examined to see if it contains a plan of which the action may be an instantiation. This particular link is sought because the syntactic rules of explanation require actions to be explained by plans. Of course, since only certain actions can be the instantiation of certain plans, a knowledge base of known plan-action instantiations must be consulted to determine whether a connection exists.

Suppose no such link can be found. Then the knowledge base of plan-action instantiations must be consulted again to see what plans this action is known to instantiate, independent of the story. If none is known, the explanation process fails. However, if some are found, these plans are hypothesized as possible explanations.

Then explanations for each plan are sought. Since the syntax of explanations requires plans to be explained by goals, such goals are sought in the story representation. Again, this requires a knowledge base that relates goals to applicable plans. If such an association is found, the process can terminate. Otherwise goals consistent with the plan to be explained are hypothesized. Goals can be explained either by themes or by plans for which they fulfill preconditions, so such items are searched for. Here knowledge bases are required that relate particular goals to particular themes and to particular plans. Since plans may be related to yet additional goals, chains of indeterminate length may be computed in this explanation process.

While explanation works backwards from the input toward an item in the representation, sometimes the presence of an item may strongly suggest a subsequent input. For example, a person who is hungry is apt to have the goal of satisfying that hunger. Thus, upon hearing of hunger, the reader might hypothesize that a goal of satisfying hunger exists. This is a form of forward inference in which prior inputs predict future ones. The advantage of forward inference is that very likely possibilities can be suggested and checked before the more general search for an explanation is begun.

To do so, the algorithm given so far need only be modified as follows: After explaining an input, the reader checks its knowledge base to see if any facts are stored associating the input with a logically subsequent part of the plan, e.g., themes with goals or goals with plans. If so, these are kept on a list of predictions. When the next input is read, it will first be matched against these predictions. If a match occurs, the input is considered to be accounted for. Otherwise, the explanation process continues, checking the predictions at the start of each cycle.

Presumably only a very few, highly probable candidates will be indexed in this manner. Of course, the more the text to be processed can be accounted for in this manner, the closer it conforms to a steretypical situation. If each subsequent event is accurately predicted, the reader has in effect done script application. Since this form of understanding is not central to our concerns here, the role of forward inferencing in speeding up the explanation process is not emphasized. The explanation process is summarized in Fig. 5.1.

Consider the processing of the following story, taken from (Schank and Abelson, 1977):

(5- 6) *Willa was hungry. She picked up the Michelin guide.*

Since the first sentence is not an action, plan, or goal, an explanation for it is not sought. However, a forward inference associated with hunger would generate the

The Process of Finding an Explanation for an Event   **Figure 5.1**

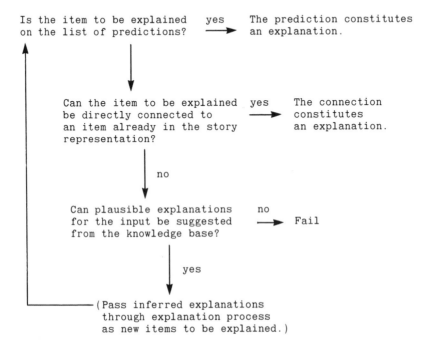

prediction that Willa has the goal of satisfying her hunger. However, this hypothesis does not directly predict the next sentence. Thus the reader must explain why Willa picked up the Michelin guide. There is no plan already in the story representation to which this action may be directly related, so the knowledge base must be consulted. The knowledge base contains the fact that picking up something is a plan for possessing that thing. So the reader hypothesizes that Willa must have had the goal of possessing the Michelin guide. This goal must then be explained. Again, there is no ready explanation for this in the story text. However, the knowledge base contains that fact that having possession of something that has a function is instrumental to performing that function. Thus the reader infers Willa was going to read the guide. Reading is often a plan for finding out some information, and since the Michelin guide is a source of information about the location of restaurants, the reader infers that Willa must have had the goal of knowing the location of a restaurant. Having this goal can be explained by the fact that knowing the location of a place is often instrumental to going there. Being at a restaurant is in turn instrumental to eating at the restaurant. Eating at a restaurant is a plan to satisfy hunger, which was previously predicted to be one of Willa's goals. An explanation for Willa's action has been found, and the inference process ceases.

This notion of explanation and the explanation process just described are incomplete in a number of ways. In particular, they do not account for more complicated kinds of explanation, such as those that involve a number of goals and the interactions between them. We shall show later on how this simple model can be extended to apply to these more complicated situations.

5.2 NONINTENTIONAL EXPLANATIONS

Explanation-driven understanding is not completely intentional in nature. It is often the case that the explanation process may be terminated when a familiar goal is inferred, even if the explanation is incomplete according to the preceding formulation. For example, if a reader were told that John was on his way to school, the reader would probably not find it necessary to explain why John was going to school. The reader would be satisfied with inferring that John was a schoolboy and with the explanation that this is simply what schoolboy's do. Of course, an intentional explanation conforming to the suggested structure is still quite possible. That is, John might go to school to please his mother or to get an education. But it is unlikely to be necessary to infer explanations at such depths in understanding ordinary texts.

One way of viewing this situation is as another example of ''short-circuiting.'' In particular, the existence of a ''normal'' event or goal or plan short circuits the explanation search by providing a canned explanation. Thus we need not compute an explanation of why John goes to school if we know this to be normal. In this case, a stored explanation for this event should be available from memory.

While the intricacies of such explanation-computation are important, we will not dwell on them here. Rather, we will concentrate on the intentional structures required for both newly computed and previously stored explanations.

5.3 PAM

This model of explanation has been used as the basis of a computer program called PAM (Plan Applier Mechanism) that can understand a number of story texts. PAM has knowledge about the kinds of plans and goals people have, and uses this knowledge in accordance with the preceding algorithm to find explanations for the events described in a text. PAM can then paraphrase the text from the points of view of the different characters in the text, as well as answer questions about the text.

For example, PAM can read the Michelin guide story (5-6), answer a number of questions about the story, and produce a paraphrase from Willa's point of view:

Input text:
> WILLA WAS HUNGRY.
> SHE PICKED UP THE MICHELIN GUIDE
> AND GOT INTO HER CAR.

Input: WHY DID WILLA PICK UP THE MICHELIN GUIDE?
Output: BECAUSE WILLA WANTED TO KNOW WHERE A RESTAURANT WAS.
Input: WHY DID WILLA GET INTO HER CAR?
Output: BECAUSE WILLA WANTED TO GET TO A RESTAURANT.
Input: WHAT WERE THE CONSEQUENCES OF WILLA PICKING UP THE MICHELIN GUIDE?
Output: THIS ENABLED WILLA TO READ THE MICHELIN GUIDE.
Output: THE STORY FROM WILLA'S POINT OF VIEW:
> I WANTED TO GET SOMETHING TO EAT, BUT I DIDN'T KNOW WHERE A RESTAURANT WAS. SO I PICKED UP THE MICHELIN GUIDE, AND I GOT INTO MY CAR.

The question-answering and paraphrasing demonstrate some of the inferences that PAM makes as it reads the story. For example, PAM has to infer that Willa was going to eat at a restaurant, that she picked up the guide in order to read it, that she read the guide to find out where a restaurant was, and that she wanted to know where one was so she could get there. PAM makes these inferences in the course of finding an explanation for Willa's action of picking up the Michelin Guide.

Actually, the name PAM is used here as a generic term denoting a number of quite different computer programs that include an implementation of the explanation algorithm given in this chapter. In the most recent version of PAM, called FAUSTUS, the explanation algorithm does not appear as a distinct process. Rather, it is implemented in terms of a number of more general knowledge manipulation primitives that are also used to simultaneously implement five additional aspects of text comprehension. These other aspects of text comprehension, along with the knowledge manipulation primitives used to implement them in FAUSTUS, are discussed in Chapter 12, together with previous implementations of PAM.

5.4 UNDERSTANDING AND META-PLANNING

PAM can understand a number of texts that are considerably more complicated than this one. These include texts that involve multiple goals and characters, revisions of plans, the abandonment of goals, and the like. The problem with such stories is that they do not obviously fall into the paradigm of simple explanation-based understanding just given. For example, suppose a character in a story had two goals that were in conflict, and took some action to resolve the conflict. The preceding model explains an action by relating it to a goal that it may help to fulfill. However, it does not immediately show how to explain an action that does not derive from a single goal, but from an attempt to mediate between two goals. To extend the explanation model to such situations, the meta-planning structures introduced in the previous chapter are required.

For example, consider the case discussed in the last chapter in which a planner is trying to get the morning newspaper without getting wet. Suppose that an understander is trying to comprehend a version of this situation in which the planner decides to stay inside and listen to the news on the radio. Without introducing meta-planning entities, we cannot explain why the planner changed its mind about getting the newspaper—the explanation for this action involves understanding that the change of plan is a way of resolving a negative interaction between two goals, and the explanation mechanism currently has no way of considering two goals at once in proposing an explanation.

This problem is resolved if the situation is considered in terms of its meta-planning structure. Recall that in our meta-planning analysis, this situation is considered to be composed of an instance of the meta-goal *RESOLVE-GOAL-CONFLICT*, and of the *TRY-ALTERNATE-PLAN* meta-plan for this meta-goal, in addition to the two ordinary goals of learning the news and not getting wet. The meta-goal, in turn, is initiated by the **ACHIEVE AS MANY GOALS AS POSSIBLE** meta-theme. The change of plan that eluded explanation earlier can now be explained by constructing this analysis. That is, the change of plan is an action that is explained by the *TRY-ALTERNATE-PLAN* meta-plan. This meta-plan is explained by the *RESOLVE-GOAL-CONFLICT* meta-goal, which in turn is explained by the meta-theme and the goal conflict situation that invoked this theme.

Thus the same model of explanation-driven understanding given in the beginning of this chapter is used to explain this more complicated situation. The only difference is that, in addition to building an explanation solely in terms of ordinary goals, part of the explanation constructed consists of meta-planning elements as well. We need only supply PAM with the appropriate meta-planning entities, and the basic explanation mechanism will apply to these more complicated situations.

Examples of more complex stories that PAM can process, as well as a description of the implementation of PAM, are found in the final chapters. However, the details of meta-planning and of goal interactions still must be formalized, for the purpose of both understanding and planning in complex situations. The theoretical apparatus for doing so is developed in the remaining chapters of this book.

6

Goal Relationships

6.1 INTRODUCTION

As was demonstrated in previous chapters, a major constraint on the theories of planning and understanding is that goals rarely occur in isolation. People often find themselves in situations in which they possess several goals simultaneously, either because they have more than one goal initially, or because the execution of a plan for a single goal impinges upon other goals that have previously remained tacit. Thus a planner must be capable of taking into account the interactions between goals in order to produce a reasonable plan. A reader must do likewise in order to arrive at a cogent explanation for someone else's behavior.

For the theory of plans to accommodate such processes, it must embody an understanding of the nature of goal interactions. Such an understanding includes an enumeration of the possible kinds of goal interactions, along with the circumstances during which each type of interaction may arise. Furthermore, knowledge about the consequences of each interaction must be specified, and most important, knowledge about possible ways of dealing with these consequences must be incorporated.

In addition, many situations involve more than one character. Each character's individual goals may interact with the goals of other characters. Because a character's plans may be affected positively or negatively by the actions of other characters, the planning process of an individual operating in interpersonal situations must take into account the actions and presumed motives of other planners.

The relationships and interactions (I use the terms interchangeably) among characters' goals and plans play an important role in determining a character's actions. To create a plan for a goal in a given situation, a planner must take into account the relation of its goal to its other goals and to the suspected goals of others. To comprehend a situation, an understander must be able to analyze the goals of the characters operating in that situation, determine the kinds of interactions that are likely, and interpret the behavior of the characters in terms of these interactions.

In this chapter, I introduce a number of goal relationships that underlie many commonplace situations, and which are useful for organizing knowledge to understand such situations or to plan in them. Each goal relationship is examined more fully in succeeding chapters, which include, for each relationship, a typology within that relationship, a description of planning tactics and related considerations, and an analysis of the relationship and associated stratagems within the meta-planning framework.

6.2 THE NEED FOR A TAXONOMY OF GOAL RELATIONSHIPS

The classification of goal relationships presented here is derived primarily from what appears to me to be logical properties inherent in these relationships. For example, some relationships involve goals within an individual, and some involve goals across different individuals. Thus this internal-external dichotomy is mirrored in the classification. However, there are many such distinctions, and from a logical point of view, there does not appear to be any principled reason to select one over another as a primary organizational element. Since the choice of emphasis seems arbitrary with respect to logical structure, I have tried to create a taxonomy that somehow parallels the organization people manifest in reasoning about complex situations. Thus, where it is possible, categories are justified by their pragmatic function in organizing knowledge about interactions in a manner useful for planning and understanding. Where this is not possible, justification is left to intuitive appeal.

Similar to the case of meta-entity organization, the content of the theory of goal interactions consists more of the details of the knowledge pertaining to particular kinds of interactions than in the overarching classification. I suspect that most of this content would be preserved if a somewhat different organization were imposed upon it. Thus the organization is more of an expositional device than it is a crucial claim of the theory.

Above all, the taxonomy must be amenable to the contraints of the understanding and planning tasks. During understanding, a system must be able to infer a goal interaction when one is likely, and then to use the presence of that goal interaction to explain a character's behavior. Similarly, in plan construction, a system may have to spot flaws in its plans that result from unforeseen goal interactions, and then have some way of rectifying these problems.

A taxonomy of goal interactions should be useful in all these tasks. For it to be so, the analysis of each type of goal interaction must include the following items:

1. A description of the various situations in which the relationship is said to exist.

2. A set of strategies that are applicable to each situation.

3. Situations that may develop from each situation, as a function of the application of some strategy or of independent events.

The first item is needed to infer the presence of the goal interaction. The second is needed to decide on a course of action given such an interaction, or to arrive at an explanation for someone else's action. The third is needed to reason about the consequences of the interaction and of one's plan to deal with it.

In sum, the taxonomy that follows is meant to be evaluated by several criteria. It should be logically accurate and consistent. It should be a useful organizational tool. Finally, it should have intuitive plausibility and naturalness.

6.3 KINDS OF GOAL RELATIONSHIPS

The relationships into which goals may enter can be categorized along several dimensions. The first dimension of categorization is based on ownership of the goals. Two categories are defined by considering the class of relationships that exists among the goals of a single individual and the class of relationships that exists among goals of different individuals. The first class is called *internal goal relationships* and the second is *external goal relationships.*

A second important distinction concerns the nature of the interaction—whether it is favorable or unfavorable. In the case of internal goal relationships, unfavorable interactions are called *goal conflicts.* Here the goals of a single individual interact in such a way that they inhibit each other's successful fulfillment. For example, a goal conflict exists if a person has the goals of both enjoying a large meal and losing weight, because the pursuit of each goal is likley to have an adverse effect on the outcome of the other.

The goals of an individual can enter into a favorable relationship with one another if the goals or their plans are similar enough so that a plan for both goals is more efficient than the plans for each goal considered separately. This situation is termed *goal overlap.* For example, a person would have overlapping goals if he wanted both to get a new toothbrush and to pick up a bottle of aspirin, and both these objects could be obtained at the same location. That is, it is easier to execute one plan that involves purchasing both objects at the same time than two plans that would require separate trips.

When an unfavorable relationship occurs between goals that belong to different individuals, the resulting situation is called *goal competition.* For example, if both John and Bill have the goal of marrying Mary, the fulfillment of one of their goals would preclude the fulfillment of the other's. Goal competition is similar to goal conflict in nature, but because it involves goals of different individuals, the situations to which it gives rise are markedly distinct. Goal competition includes a class of interactions across planners that is treated in detail by Carbonell (1979).

A favorable interaction among the goals of different individuals in called *goal concord.* Goal concord occurs when the same goal is shared by different agents. If England and France both have the goal of defeating Germany, for example, then these goals would be in concord. As a result, the agents involved are likely to help each other achieve various subtasks that would not otherwise be each other's concern.

The categorization of goal relationships is summarized in Table 6.1. Each of the categories is further analyzed into subcategories in subsequent chapters.

As this categorization of goal relationships is along multiple dimensions, it does not lend itself well to a linear presentation. The chapters that follow are designed to capture those generalizations that appear to be most significant in structuring the knowledge needed for reasoning about these relationships. Many of the structures that give rise to internal negative goal relationships appear similar to those that give rise to external negative goal relationships; however, the strategies applicable in each case are quite different. Thus the structure of both kinds of negative goal relationships is discussed in one chapter; the situations to which each gives rise are treated separately. The situation is analogous for positive goal relationships, which are covered in a like fashion.

6.4 SOME TERMINOLOGY

In talking about relationships between goals, we must often distinguish between those goals that just happen to co-occur and those that co-exist because they are involved in some common task. For example, if John wants to play racquetball, he needs to have a racquet he can use, and he must have a court and a partner available. However, all these goals are instrumental to his playing and thus should be considered part of the same task.

We refer to a set of plans and goals possessed by one character and derived from the same purpose as a *task network*. The task network also includes the explicit representation of the relations between these components. For example, suppose John wants to chat with Mary and also wants to eat, and that they decide to go to a restaurant together. This situation involves a number of goals and plans. John has

Classification of Goal Relationships Table 6.1

	Negative Interactions	Positive Interactions
Internal Goal Relationships	Goal Conflict: Mutually opposing goals held by one individual.	Goal Overlap: Goals that are achieved more easily together than apart.
External Goal Relationships	Goal Competition: Mutually opposing goals held by different individuals.	Goal Concord: The same goal possessed by several individuals.

the goal of eating, and his plan for this goal is to eat at a restaurant. Instrumental to this goal is the goal of being at a restaurant. John also wants to talk to Mary, and instrumental to this is that he be near her. Thus there are at least two task networks interacting here. One contains the plans and goals involved in John's getting fed, and another contains the plans and goals involved in John's side of having a chat with Mary. In addition, Mary probably is operating under a number of goals of her own, each of which would be associated with its own task network.

The task networks involved in each of these cases may be of a larger scope than previously suggested. For example, John's goal of eating probably derives from a need to satisfy his hunger or a desire for enjoyment. He may also have some purpose for wanting to talk to Mary. The task network includes these higher level goals and themes, as well as lower level goals that may be sprouted as the plans are executed. Of course, the task network needs to represent the facts that some particular goal arises from the need to fulfill a precondition for some particular plan, that some theme gives rise to a certain goal, that a plan is aimed at achieving a particular goal, and so on.

Subtasks are portions of a task network that stem from the same goal. For example, in order for John to chat with Mary, he might have to arrange a meeting and then go to it. Each of these subgoals generates a task network. The subgoal of arranging the meeting might give rise to a network involving making a telephone call and finding out Mary's number, whereas the subgoal of being at the meeting would include the goals involved in using an automobile. Each connected set of plans and goals that can be traced to a common subgoal is a subtask network.

The concept of a task network is useful in discussing goal relationships for two reasons. First, if two goals are in some relationship to one another, the other goals in their respective task networks often take on a relationship. For example, if two goals are in conflict, this may mean that the other goals and plans in their task networks are also in conflict. Thus we can talk about a conflict between two goals that exists not between the goals themselves, but between goals in their respective task networks.

Task networks also provide a way of talking about multiple occurrences of the same goal or plan. If a goal is instrumental to two different plans, or if it is generated by two themes, we may want to describe the goal as occurring twice, even though only one actual goal exists. However, this state of affairs is easily described using the notion of a task network simply by saying that the same goal partakes in two different task networks. Thus a task network provides a convenient way of referring to the themes, goals, plans, and actions currently being considered by a planner, and of the relationships between elements.

7

Negative Goal Relationships

7.1 INTRODUCTION

Negative goal relationships are goal interactions that cause difficulties for the planners involved. For example, consider the following stories.

(7- 1) *John wanted to watch the Monday night football game. He also had a paper due the next day. That night, John watched the football game. John failed Civics.*

(7- 2) *John wanted to marry Mary. He also wanted to marry Sue. John took Mary out and proposed to her. She agreed. Later, John called Sue and told her he wouldn't be seeing her anymore.*

These stories each contain several goals. These goals are not independent of one another, as is demonstrated by the fact that the stories cannot be understood by following each goal separately. There is no intrinsic reason that watching a football game should cause one to fail a course, as it did in story (7-1). Nor can one explain why John no longer wanted to see somebody he was considering marrying in story (7-2).

However, explanations for the events in these stories are readily inferred: In (7-1) John spent too much time watching the football game, so he didn't have enough time left to write his paper. In (7-2) John decided to marry Mary, so he had to give up seeing other women. In each case, the explanation for a character's behavior is a function not of a single goal, but of an interaction between two goals.

The relationship of the goals in story (7-1) and those in story (7-2) is called *goal conflict*. A goal conflict is defined as a situation in which a character has several goals at the same time, and the fulfillment of one of these goals interferes with the fulfillment of the others. A person's goals can also be adversely affected by goals possessed by other characters. For example, consider the following stories.

(7- 3) *John told Mary he wanted to watch the football game. Mary said that she wanted to watch the Bolshoi ballet. Mary put on channel 3. John got out the lawnmower.*

(7- 4) *John wanted to win the high hurdles. Bill also wanted to win the high hurdles. John won the race. Bill was very upset.*

As in the case of goal conflict, stories (7-3) and (7-4) cannot be understood without realizing that the characters' goals are related. The relationship between the different characters' goals in these stories is called *goal competition*. This refers to those situations in which the fulfillment of one character's goal precludes the fulfillment of another's. These examples illustrate the role of goal competition in constructing the explanations necessary for text understanding. Its role in the planning process is analogous.

Goals that are in a negative relationship to one another are in danger of failing to be achieved or of being abandoned. A planner whose own goals are in conflict may therefore try to alter a plan or eliminate the cause of the conflict, or it may have to postpose fulfillment of a goal or give up one of them entirely. Planners whose goals compete with one another may adopt similar strategies. In addition, these planners have the option of using a set of planning strategies specifically designed to deal with opposition. These plans aimed at undermining an opponent are called *anti-plans*.

In story understanding, the recognition of goal conflict or goal competition provides a powerful predictive function. A reader who detects a negative goal relationship can expect a character to act in a manner to rid himself of the conflict, or else the reader can expect a goal to fail. Thus knowledge about goal conflict and competition is needed to explain the behavior of a character who finds himself in such a situation.

In addition, negative goal relationships create problems for a character as they adversely affect the chances of a goal being fulfilled. These adverse conditions constitute a dramatic component that many stories are centered about. Thus the structure of the content of a story is often a function of the negative goal interactions present in the story, and of the situations to which these interactions give rise. A story understander will remember such situations as the *points* of the story (Wilensky, 1980).

In planning, the recognition of a negative goal relationship by a planner is important for generating a reasonable plan. For example, a planner faced with a goal conflict may have to decide which of the conflicting goals is less important and should be abandoned. A planner in a goal competition situation may have to determine his opponent's strategy and then select a plan to counter it. Or he may have to realize that his opponent is executing a plan directed against him and try to counter that plan.

While goal conflict and goal competition are very different situations, the subcategories into which they may be divided are quite similar. These categories serve to organize the knowledge needed to detect the interactions when they occur, and to reason about the situations to which they give rise. The presentation in this chapter is biased toward goal conflict, with examples of goal competition also given, along with the modifications necessary for the categories to apply to the goals of different individuals. Unless it is otherwise noted, what is stated about the structure of goal conflict applies to goal competition as well.

Goal conflict and goal competition may be subject o similar categorization, and the situations to which they give rise are highly similar along certain dimensions. However, the strategies for dealing with these situations are quite different in some respects. For example, goal competition situations involve dealing with an adversary, and thus admit a set of planning considerations specific to dealing with other planners. Such considerations do not arise in goal conflicts, where only one character is involved.

In addition, goal conflict and goal competition have rather different statuses with respect to the overall theory of plans. Briefly, goal conflict considerations must be incorporated explicitly into the theory of plans because knowing what to do in the presence of a set of goals is basic to the functioning of an individual planner. Goal competition considerations, on the other hand, have no such elevated status. Rather, they simply constitute knowledge about what to do when the situation happens to involve another planning agent. For these reasons, the strategies applicable to goal conflict and goal competition are discussed separately in subsequent chapters.

7.2 KINDS OF GOAL CONFLICT AND COMPETITION

To understand a story or act in a situation involving a negative goal relationship, a reader or planner must be able to recognize that the relationship is present and then reason about that relationship. These tasks require the exact nature of that relationship to be taken into account. The following is an exposition of the knowledge needed for these tasks, presented in the form of a classification of types of negative goal relationships.

Goal conflict or goal competition occurs when planners desire to bring into existence states that exclude one another. However, the nature of these states and their relation to the goals in question may vary considerably. It is useful to distinguish three classes of negative goal relationships:

1. Resource Limitations—Two goals are in a negative relationship to one another when the plans for the goals require a common resource, and there is an insufficient quantity of that resource available for both plans. For example, not having enough time or money may limit the set of goals one can fulfill, thus causing a conflict among those goals. Similarly, if two planners need the same resource, their goals may be in competition with one another.

2. Mutually Exclusive States—States involved in the fulfillment of different goals may simply be incompatible with one another. For example, two goals may require the planner to be in two different places at once, thus causing a conflict for that planner. Two different planners may have goals that require exclusive states to exist, thus putting their goals in competition.

3. Causing a Preservation Goal—Executing the plan for one goal can cause a preservation goal to come into being, thus creating a conflict between the original goal and the preservation goal. For example, taking the day off to go fishing may cost one one's job, creating a conflict between enjoying oneself and remaining employed. Similarly, if one person's smoking annoys another, goal competition exists between the former's goal of enjoying oneself and the latter's goal of preventing the unpleasant experience of being exposed to cigarette smoke.

Several caveats are in order about this classification. First, it fails to distinguish between proper goal conflicts and what might be termed ''plan conflicts.'' In the latter case, the conflict arises not through the nature of the goals themselves but through the plans selected to achieve these goals. For example, resource shortages occur because the plans chosen for the goals just happen to consume the same resource, while the goals themselves have no intrinsic relationship.

However, I prefer to label as goal conflicts all situations in which the pursuit of one goal interferes with another, regardless of whether the conflict is intrinsic to the goals or not. This is useful because some general processes apply to all goal conflicts so defined. In addition, it seems that people generally do recognize a conflict as independent of its true basis. In any case, many distinctions within the category of goal conflict are based on the cause of the goal conflict, and thus the differences that result are not neglected (however, see Carbonell, 1979, for a somewhat different formulation).

A second caveat concerns the basic division into the three categories of negative goal relationships. Strictly speaking, all goal conflicts might be termed mutually exclusive states. For example, a resource shortage may be formulated as: ''The state of plan P1 using resource R and the state of plan P2 also using resource R are mutually exclusive.'' However, I find this statement to be awkward and counter-intuitive, and feel that there are real differences in how one cognizes these situations. However, the issue is largely one of terminology. Regardless of how the analysis is phrased, we need to make the distinctions presented here at some point because each gives rise to a goal conflict that functions differently.

7.3 RESOURCE LIMITATIONS

A *resource* is something needed to perform a plan. Thus a goal conflict situation can result when plans for a set of goals require a common resource which is available in an insufficient quantity for all the proposed plans. The following stories contain examples of goal conflicts caused by a shortage of resources.

(7- 5)   *John had just enough money to buy either a television or a stereo, but he wanted to have both.*

(7- 6)   *John wanted to cook linguine and hamburgers on his camp stove, but the stove had only one burner.*

(7- 7)   *John wanted to watch the football game, but he had a paper due the next day.*

Each of these situations contains a conflict involving a different class of resource. Each class of resource has salient properties that contribute to goal conflicts in different ways, and which therefore merit closer scrutiny. For example, story (7-5) involves a shortage of money, a resource that is used up in the process of being used. The conflict in story (7-6) is based on the use of an object that is not consumed, but whose properties limit its capacity. Finally, in story (7-7), the scarce resource is time, which has its own peculiar properties.

A resource shortage can cause the goals of several planners to compete with one another as well. For example, consider the following stories:

(7- 8) *John and Bill were driving across the desert when their car broke down. They had only enough water left for one of them to make it to the nearest town.*

(7- 9) *John wanted to watch the football game on television, but Mary wanted to watch the Bolshoi ballet.*

These examples involve an object that is consumed or one that provides a functional capacity. For reasons to be discussed shortly, there is no analog to time-based conflicts among competitive goals.

Resource-based negative goal interactions are more truly conflicts between the plans for the goals than between the goals themselves. For example, in story (7-7), John might decide to hire someone to write his paper for him, or he might try to record the game on a video-recorder and watch it at some later time. In either case, the two goals in the story would both be accomplished, demonstrating that the conflict is based on the plans chosen for those goals rather than on any intrinsic property of the goals themselves.

Nevertheless, a reader of story (7-7) would most likely perceive a conflict solely on the mention of the goals. This is because the reader infers the *normal plans* for each goal, unless there is information to the contrary, and then infers the goal conflict based on the nature of these plans. Similarly, a planner seeking to fulfill one of these goals would most likely first consider such a normal plan before realizing the difficulties entailed by its use. Since readers or planners seem to infer such conflicts based only on the existence of the goals, and because plan-based conflicts function similarly to true goal conflicts in other ways, I include these interactions in the category of goal conflict rather than introducing a separate plan-conflict category. Although to consider plan-based goal conflicts and true goal conflicts as constituting one natural category seems plausible, it does lead to some asymmetries which we will discuss more fully.

As the preceding examples illustrate, there are several different kinds of conflict based on resource shortages, because different resources function in different ways. For the purposes of understanding goal relationships and, in fact, for understanding planning in general, we can distinguish the following classes of resources.

1. Time—The plans for all goals require some time to be executed. Thus time plays a pervasive role in causing goal conflicts. Time is a rather unique resource in that it is available equally to all planners. A planner cannot obtain more of it or less of it, and it is consumed whether it is used or not.

2. Consumable Functional Objects—Unlike time, most resources tend to have narrower applicability. A resource that is normally used for a particular plan is called a *functional object*. A consumable, functional object is one whose use to the planner is reduced when it is used. For example, money is a functional object that is normally used for trading. It is consumable because it is no longer available to the planner after he buys something with it. Functional objects differ from time in several other ways: one planner may possess more of the resource that another; it is possible to obtain more of the resource or to squander it; and it is not continuously renewed. The notion of consumption determines the amount of use a resource can be to a planner. Consumable resources are involved in goal conflicts when the amount of the resource needed by the planner exceeds the amount available to the planner.

3. Nonconsumable Functional Objects—A nonconsumable functional object is one that is not used up when it takes part in a plan. For example, in story (7-6), the stove is a nonconsumable functional object; after it is used by the planner, it may be used by him again. Although nonconsumable functional objects are not used up in a plan, they limit their utility to the planner through their capacity. That is, they can only provide so much of a function over a fixed period of time. Nonconsumable functional objects therefore give rise to goal conflicts when they are available to a planner in a capacity that is more limited than is needed.

4. Abilities—An ability is the extent to which a character can perform an action, for example a person's strength, speed, intellect, how good he is at a particular skill, his stamina, and so on. Abilities differ from individual to individual; they usually cannot be changed over short periods of time, although they are amenable to long-term plans. Unlike functional objects, they are more likely to deteriorate with disuse than with use. Like nonconsumable functional objects, abilities have capacities and are likely to lead to goal conflicts when this capacity is exceeded by the demand for it.

Of course, there are dimensions to resources other than these. For example, we have not discussed the notion of a perishable resource, or the fact that nonconsumable functional objects may wear out instead of being consumed. Although these characteristics are important for planning, it is our list of the four categories of resources that seems to play a key role in producing negative goal relationships.

Note that in the case competition, the resource must be, in principle, sharable. That is, the parties involved must have access to the same resource in order for the conflict to exist. This is possible for some types of resources, but not for others. For example, most functional objects are sharable, as they can be used by any planner, but time and abilities are not transferable. That is, we cannot use someone else's time or take direct advantage of their abilities. Thus while there are goal conflicts involving all these types of resources and goal competition involving functional objects, we cannot base goal competition on nonsharable resources such as time or abilities.

7.3.1 Time

All plans require some amount of time to be executed. A goal conflict based on a limitation of time resources is therefore possible whenever a character is actively pursuing more than one goal. In order to have a conflict involving a scarcity of time, two conditions must be met:

1. *It must be necessary to execute both plans during the same period of time.*
2. *The simultaneous execution of both plans cannot be feasible.*

The first condition states that there can be no way to arrange the executions of both plans so that they do not overlap. A period of time during which a plan is to be executed is called its *time window*. Thus the time windows of the two plans must overlap for there to be a time-based resource shortage. For this to happen, each plan must be required to start at a certain time, and each plan must last long enough so that assigning them nonoverlapping time windows is not possible.

Restrictions on where the time windows for a plan can be placed can come from one of two sources:

1. The goal with which the plan is associated may include a deadline by which the goal must be fulfilled.
2. The plan may have to be synchronized with some external event.

An example of the first would be the goal of handing in an assignment for a course that has a due date; an example of the second would be the goal of wanting to take a photograph of the moon, for which a planner must synchronize his actions with the period of the moon's visibility. In either case, there is a time interval within which the execution of the plan must be begun if it is to have any possibility of succeeding. We call such a slot of time *an interval of initiation.*

Thus we can think of a plan as being constrained to start within a particular interval of initiation. The interval of initiation of a plan affects the intervals of initiation of its subplans and of its parent plans as well. As a subgoal must be achieved prior to the achievement of its parent, restrictions on the time of initiation of the parent restrict the latest possible time of initiation of the subplan; restrictions on the time of initiation of the subplan restrict the earliest possible time of initiation of the parent. In general, we distinguish between *internal* and *external* restrictions on a plan, the internal being those inherent in the plan itself, and external referring to restrictions derived from a relation to another goal, such as a subgoal or parent goal. If a plan within a task network is internally constrained to start within some interval, it may constrain other plans in its task network to start within some interval.

Given the intervals of initiation for the task networks associated with a pair of goals, a necessary condition for a goal conflict is that *any possible time window for one of the goals entirely include the interval of initiation of the other.* If this were not the case, it would be possible to initiate one plan after the completion of the other. Figure 7.1 illustrates this principle with a few examples.

In Fig. 7.1 the straight lines represent possible time windows, i.e., the proposed periods of plan execution. The bounded regions represent intervals of initiation, or possible starting times for the plans. In each case two different plans are scheduled. For example, A shows that one plan is scheduled to be started near the beginning of its interval of initiation, and the other toward the middle of its interval. This allows enough time for both plans to be run serially, as the nonoverlapping arrangement of the dotted lines indicates. A similar situation occurs in C. In B and D, however, one time window must completely cover the interval of

Time Constraints Causing Goal Conflicts   **Figure 7.1**

```
        Plan 1 Execution

        ───────────────────── Plan 2 Execution

  A     └─────────────┘      ──────────          No forced overlap

            I.I.1      └──────────────┘
                           I.I. 2



        Plan 1 Execution

        ─────────────────────────────

                          Plan 2 Execution

  B     └─────────────┘      ──────────          Forced overlap

            I.I.1      └──────────────┘
                           I.I. 2



        Plan 1 Execution        Plan 2 Execution

        ──────────────────     ──────────  No forced overlap

  C     └─────────────┘          └────┘

            I.I. 1                 I.I. 2



                          Plan 2 Execution

        Plan 1 Execution    ──────

        ──────────────────              Forced overlap

  D     └─────────────┘  └──┘

            I.I. 1            I.I. 2


  ─────────────────────────────────────►
                time
```

initiation of the other, thus precluding a mutually satisfactory arrangement.

In addition to the task networks being constrained to fit into overlapping time windows, for there to be a time-based goal conflict, the planner must be incapable of successfully executing both plans simultaneously. In order to preclude simultaneous execution of a set of plans, one of three conditions must hold. The simultaneous execution of the plans:

1. *May be beyond an ability of the planner.*
2. *May be beyond the capacity of a nonconsumable functional object required by both plans.*
3. *May require two mutually exclusive states coming into existence.*

That is, the need for some resource involved in the execution of both plans must be strained sufficiently so that both plans cannot be executed adequately, or the resulting situation is simply not feasible.

The following stories illustrate how these factors contribute to goal conflicts involving time:

(7-10) John had to do his topology problem set, but he also wanted to play poker with the boys.
(7-11) John wanted to chat with Mary, but his train left in five minutes.
(7-12) John wanted to simmer two dishes on his camp stove, but the stove had only one burner.

Each example requires two plans to be executed at once. This cannot be done, but for different reasons in each case. In story (7-10), a lack of an *ability* is the problem; John does not have enough *attention* capacity to perform both plans effectively at once. To see that the role of abilities is prevalent here, note that the goal conflict would not exist in the following situation:

(7-13) John wanted to eat some pretzels, but he also wanted to play poker with the boys.

Here the example is surprising because it leads us to expect a goal conflict that does not exist. The conflict is not present here because, unlike story (7-10), the attention capacity required is small enough to permit execution of both plans at once.

In story (7-11), being on a train prohibits communicating with Mary at the same time, an instance of mutually exclusive states. John would be required to be in two places at once to converse with Mary and still catch his train (assuming of course that she is not going with him). Hence the conflict arises from the need to bring two such exclusive states into existence at once. In story (7-12), it is the capacity of a functional object that is inadequate to support the plans for both goals simultaneously. If the capacity were increased, say, by supplying another burner, then presumably both goals could be fulfilled by plans executed concurrently.

Conflicts based on space fall into this category. While time merits a special category, space is treated as a capacity of some functional object, rather than as an autonomous entity. Space is therefore not delegated a privileged position in this analysis and is handled as any other functional capacity of an object.

In sum, time-based conflicts occur when the plans for the goals must be scheduled so that they overlap and when these plans cannot be executed simultaneously. For the plans to be forced to overlap, the goals must either have a time constraint built in, or they must have to be synchronized with an external event. For them not to be executable simultaneously, they must either require mutually exclusive states to come into existence, be beyond the capacity of a functional object, or be beyond the capability of the planner.

7.3.2 Consumable Objects

A *consumable object* is a functional object whose use to the planner is reduced after it performs its function. An insufficient quantity of a consumable can therefore cause a negative goal interaction as the execution of one plan may deprive another plan of a prerequisite resource. Different consumable objects are consumed differently, leading to a diversity of situations that constitute this sort of negative goal relationship and requiring further subcategorization. With this end in mind, the following kinds of consumption are distinguished:

1. Physical Consumption—The object consumed either fails to exist after it is used in some plan, or it changes into some other substance that no longer has the desired properties.
2. Social Consumption—Control of the object is transferred away from the planner so the planner cannot use it subsequently.
3. Continuous Enablement Consumption—An object can be consumed if the goal to which it is applied requires that object to remain in a state continuously or undo the achievement of the goal. This form of causality is discussed by Rieger (1975b).

Story (7-5) is an example of a goal conflict caused by social consumption. The following stories illustrate the other two kinds.

(7-14) John had to blow up two bridges, but he only had one explosive charge left.
(7-15) John wanted to put up two posters, but he only had one thumbtack.

In story (7-14), the dynamite is destroyed as a consequence of its use, and is thus physically consumed by the plan; in story (7-15) a thumbtack must continually support a poster, so the tack is consumed by continuous enablement.

Consumption is related to but is distinct from the concept of an object wearing out. The difference is that wearing out usually refers to the functional object losing its ability to function in a way that is not inherent in its nature as a functional object. That is, a car may wear out if it is used long enough, but gasoline is consumed. The difference is that the gasoline changes in a way that is inherent in its role as a fuel, whereas it is possible, in principle, that the car could function forever without the changes that constitute wear. The concept of wearing out probably plays a similar role to consumption in long-range planning. That is, for very long-range plans, functional objects can be treated as consumable objects with wear playing the role of consumption.

Because the amount of a consumable available to an individual can change over time, considerations based on consumption may interact with time considerations. Consider the following story.

(7-16)   *John earned 30K a year. He decided he could afford either a trip to Europe or a trip to Mexico each year.*

Here the conflict is between the various vacation goals. Since John supposedly would like to take both trips each year, the goals are in conflict based on a lack of resources. In general, if the resource is available as a function of time, the conflict will depend on the time frame within which the goals are desired. Thus these are conflicts that are equally well classified as being based on a limitation of time or on a limitation of consumable resources.

In keeping with the previous section, these conflicts are classified as time-based goal conflicts in which the plans for the goals cannot be executed simultaneously because of the lack of capacity of a functional object, in this case, of a consumable one. As in all such cases, the conflict will evaporate if either more time or more of the consumable resource is obtained.

7.3.3 Mutually Exclusive States

Goals can conflict or compete due to resource limitations because of the nature of the plans chosen for each goal. In addition, goals can be inimical toward one another because achieving them would require mutually exclusive states to come into existence. In the previous section, we examined some cases of goals whose plans mutually exclude each other's concurrent execution. This section is concerned with mutual exclusion in its own right.

Consider the following stories:

(7-17)   *John wanted to have his cake and eat it, too.*
(7-18)   *John wanted to marry Mary, but Mary wanted to marry Bill.*
(7-19)   *John wanted to satisfy his hunger, but he was trying to lose weight as well.*
(7-20)   *John wanted to have a regular job. He also wanted to collect unemployment insurance.*

These stories illustrate a number of ways in which mutually exclusive states can give rise to negative goal interactions:

1. The goals themselves constitute exclusive states. Story (7-17) is an instance of such a situation causing a goal conflict. In story (7-18), the same sort of interaction causes a form of goal competition.

2. One goal state may be excluded by a state that is a consequence of a plan for another goal. For example, a consequence of eating is gaining weight, which excludes John's goal of becoming thin in story (7-19).

3. A precondition for a plan for one of the goals might exclude the other goal. This is the case in story (7-20), where not having a job is a precondition for one of John's goals, but excludes the other.

A further distinction is made between *logical exclusion* and *social exclusion*. Two states are logically exclusive if one state implies that the other state cannot exist. Specific facts about how a domain is structured are required for this task. For example, certain facts about space are required in order to understand that being in one place precludes being in a different place at the same time. Enumerating and representing a full set of such rules is an open problem, but see McDermott (1980) and Davis (1981) for some relevant efforts.

Socially exclusive states cannot exist at the same time because of cultural prohibitions. For example, John's goals in story (7-18) are socially exclusive because his society prohibits a person from being married to two people at once. Determining that two states are socially exclusive requires that the social preconditions of that state are stored along with that state.

The primary reason for distinguishing social exclusion from logical exclusion is related to how the goal conflict may be dealt with. In the case of logical exclusion, the conflict cannot be resolved without eliminating the need to bring about one of the states. In the case of social exclusion, however, it may be possible to circumvent the exclusion at the risk of violating a social convention. This violation usually has negative consequences, and therefore violating it may cause yet another goal conflict. For example, it is possible to be married to two people, but this constitutes bigamy and is illegal. Thus resolving the goal conflict involved in wanting to be married to two people at once is itself in conflict with a preservation goal of not getting arrested. Such conflicts are explored in the following section.

One particular form of goal competition based on mutually exclusive states merits a special label. This involves goals that cannot exist apart from competition with someone else's goal and thus are termed *inherently competitive* goals. For example, the goal of winning a race is inherently competitive because one cannot win a race without beating someone else who also wants to win. In contrast, story (7-18) has mutually exclusive goals that are not inherently exclusive, as someone can want to marry someone else independently of whether there is another suitor. Processing inherently competitive goals does not require any special computation, except that their appearance immediately entails a goal interaction.

Mutually exclusive states is the form of goal conflict that has received the most treatment in artificial intelligence work on planning and problem solving. For example, Sussman's celebrated "goal clobbers brother goal" critic (Sussman, 1975) detects goal conflicts of this sort. Sacerdoti's critics that deal with conflict also fall into this category (Sacerdoti, 1974).

7.3.4 Causing a Preservation Goal

Consider the following stories:

(7-21)   John wanted to go to the football game, but it was raining outside.
(7-22)   John wanted to take the night off, but he thought his boss would fire him.

Unlike most of the other stories discussed in this chapter, each of these stories has only one explicit goal in it. However, in each case, a conflict exists between the explicitly stated goal and an undesirable state that would result from the fulfillment of that goal.

Wanting to prevent an undesirable state from coming into existence is called a preservation goal (Schank and Abelson, 1977). I attribute a preservation goal to a person if and only if some particular threat to a desired state of affairs exists. In contrast, I term the general tendency to preserve such states, and thereby to have preservation goals, the preservation theme. The preservation theme is known to the Goal Detector, which consequently lies in wait for a situation in which a particular preservation goal should be detected.

Preservation goal generation may be involved in the creation of goal competition as well. Consider the following stories.

(7-23)   John asked Mary to stop smoking because the smoke annoyed him.
(7-24)   John wanted to go to the track, but his wife didn't want him to go because she thought gambling was immoral.
(7-25)   Johnny wanted an ice cream cone, but his mother thought it would spoil his appetite.

In each of these stories, one of the character's goals is caused by another character's action. Since goals so generated are to prevent an effect of the other character's action, each situation is a goal competition in which one character's goal causes another character to have a preservation goal.

Detecting these goal conflict or goal competition situations is a direct consequence of the ability to detect goals in general. For example, when a planner has a goal, it uses the Projector to hypothesize the future situation that pursuit of this goal will entail. If this hypothetical situation is undesirable, the Goal Detector will infer a preservation goal. The planner need only check that the undesirable scenario derives from one's own goal in order to determine that a goal conflict exists.

Detecting such conflicts is a basic part of one's planning ability. It allows a planner to try alternative plans for a given goal and to deal in advance with the problems that may arise when a plan is executed. In effect, preservation goals assume the role of constraints; they prevent the planner from blindly destroying what it has already created or currently enjoys in the process of achieving its next desire.

7.4   SUMMARY OF NEGATIVE GOAL RELATION CLASSIFICATION

Goals can conflict or compete with one another in a number of ways. The following classification is useful for organizing these negative goal relationships:

   1. Resource Shortages—These are further broken down according to type of resources involved. In the case of goal competition, it is also necessary that the resource be sharable.

2. Mutually Exclusive States—These include negative relationships based on socially exclusive states and on logically exclusive states. The states involved may be the actual goal states, preconditions of plans for those goals, or consequences of performing the plans.

3. Generating a Preservation Goal—These relationships contain one goal and a preservation goal that is inferred to prevent a plan for the original goal from having an adverse side effect.

8

Reasoning About Goal Conflict

8.1 INTRODUCTION

The previous chapter introduced the notions of goal conflict and goal competition. A classification for these conflicts was described, and purported to be useful for detecting the presence of negative goal relationships and for reasoning about them once they are detected. While the categorization of these goal relationships is essentially the same for competition and for conflict, the situations that arise from each type are rather different. This chapter and the next describe the knowledge needed by planners and understanders to reason about situations involving goal conflict and goal competition, respectively.

This chapter describes those situations that may develop from the presence of a goal conflict. Three types of situations are examined here: *goal conflict resolution,* in which a planner tries to resolve the goal conflict and satisfy all his goals; *goal abandonment,* in which a planner simply opts for one goal and abandons the others; and *accidental goal resolution,* in which an external event occurs that resolves the goal conflict for the planner.

Most of this chapter is concerned with the resolution of goal conflicts. I examine the general framework within which goal conflicts may be resolved and also look at some ways of resolving particular kinds of conflict. As before, I explore the use of this knowledge both from the point of view of planning, in which an attempt to resolve a conflict is sought, and from the point of view of understanding, in which a reader attempts to understand the actions of a character trying to resolve a conflict of his own. The classification of goal conflicts given in the previous chapter is used here to organize the relevant knowledge.

8.2 SITUATIONS RESULTING FROM GOAL CONFLICT

A planner or an understander needs to spot goal conflicts because doing so enables it to plan its own subsequent actions or to interpret someone else's. For example, consider the following stories:

(8- 1) *John was in a hurry to make an important business meeting. On the way over, he ran into an old girlfriend. She invited him up to her apartment and John accepted. The next day, John's boss told him he was fired.*

(8- 2) *John was in a hurry to make an important business meeting. On the way over, he ran into an old girlfriend who invited John up to her apartment. John called his boss and asked if the meeting could be postponed.*

(8- 3) *John wanted both a stereo and a television, but he only had enough money for one. John decided to take a second job.*

(8- 4) *John had just enough money to buy either a stereo or a television, but he wanted both. Then John learned he inherited a small fortune.*

These stories demonstrate a variety of situations that can arise from a goal conflict, and the role of knowledge about conflict in planning and understanding. For example, in story (8-1), a reader needs to recognize the goal conflict in order to infer the subsequent failure of one of the goals, as the failure of this goal is not explicitly mentioned in the text. In stories (8-2) and (8-3), John tries to do away with a cause of the conflict, in each case his actions depending on the class of goal conflict involved. For story (8-4), a reader needs to understand that a fortuitous circumstance freed John of his problem. Similarly, a planner faced with the same goal conflicts besetting John would have to be capable of making a number of relevant judgments based on a knowledge of goal conflict situations.

These stories are examples of three distinct classes of situations that can arise after the occurrence of a goal conflict:

1. Goal Conflict Resolution—The planner can try to resolve the conflict. Stories (8-2) and (8-3) describe attempts at goal conflict resolution. If the planner fails to resolve a conflict, it can still try the next alternative.

2. Goal Abandonment—The character can simply opt for one of the conflicting goals and try to fulfill it, abandoning the other goal. In addition, the planner might try to partially fulfill one or both goals in order to permit fulfillment of the other. Story (8-1) contains an instance of complete goal abandonment.

3. Spontaneous Goal Conflict Resolution—The conflict may be resolved by someone other than the planner or his agent. For example, in (8-4), John's inheritance eliminated one of the causes of John's goal conflict, thus making that conflict evaporate.

Each of these situations organizes knowledge about how a planner may reasonably behave in that situation. The most important of these situations is goal conflict resolution. In accordance with the meta-theme **ACHIEVE AS MANY GOALS AS POSSIBLE**, a planner faced with a goal conflict has as its first duty to try to seek some way of allowing all its goals to be achieved. Thus the presence of a goal conflict causes this meta-theme to produce the meta-goal of resolving the goal conflict. If this meta-goal fails, the meta-theme **MAXIMIZE THE VALUE OF THE GOALS ACHIEVED** is brought into play. This meta-theme causes the planner to have the meta-goal of evaluating and selecting the most valuable scenario. This would result in the abandonment of some goals and the retention of others. Finally, if the situation should change so that the cause of the conflict no longer exists, the planner needs to recognize this so that he no longer pursues the meta-goals that derive from it.

Each of these goal conflict situations is now considered in turn.

8.3 RESOLVING A GOAL CONFLICT

Since it is desirable to achieve all of one's goals, a planner faced with a goal conflict will probably attempt to resolve that conflict. I express this by saying that the state of having a goal conflict is a situation that causes the meta-theme **ACHIEVE AS MANY GOALS AS POSSIBLE** to become active. In such a situation, this theme creates the meta-goal of resolving the goal conflict. This is a meta-goal because resolving the conflict can be viewed as a planning problem that needs to be solved by the creation of a better plan. In this formulation, the resolution of the goal conflict is performed by the execution of a meta-plan, the result of which will be a set of altered plans whose execution will not interfere with one another.

The knowledge needed to replan around a goal conflict is quite diverse, and may depend on either the particular goals in question or the nature of type of the conflict. However, the meta-plans with which this knowledge is applied are rather general. To see why, it is necessary to ask how it is possible for goal conflicts to be resolved at all. That is, what properties can a situation have so that a planner will anticipate goals colliding but which still allows room to prevent a collision?

Recall that a goal conflict can come about in two ways. A conflict may be a function of the plans for one's goals. In this case, it may be possible to achieve the goals by selecting other, nonconflicting plans. Or the conflict may be inherent in the goals themselves. Changing one's plans will not relieve this situation. However, it may be that this inherent exclusion is dependent on some additional circumstance. Thus the conflict might be resolved if this circumstance is changed.

Thus there are essentially two ways of going about resolving a conflict. We can try to seek new plans for our goals or try to change the circumstances surrounding the goals that are deemed to be causing the problem. I therefore define two very general meta-plans, *REPLAN* and *CHANGE-CIRCUMSTANCE*. We now examine in some detail how these meta-plans may be used to resolve goal conflicts.

8.3.1 *REPLAN*

A number of different replanning strategies are applicable to goal conflict situations. They are given here in order of decreasing specificity. This implies an assumption about the order in which such plans would actually be used, i.e., the most specific one first, then progressively more general ones, until a satisfactory set of plans is found. In this respect, meta-plans are entirely analogous to ordinary plans insofar as the planning process is concerned, i.e., first the "normal plan" for a goal is tried, and only if a difficulty is encountered will an attempt to use more general plans be made. This ordering is merely the result of the First Law of Knowledge Application applied to the meta-level.

8.3.1.1 *USE-NORMAL-PLAN* APPLIED TO RESOLVING GOAL CONFLICTS

The most specific replanning strategy is finding a normal plan. A normal plan in the case of goal conflict is a stored plan specifically designed for use in a goal conflict between the kinds of goals found in the current situation. For example, consider the following stories.

(8- 5) *John wanted to go outside and get the newspaper, but he discovered it was raining. He got out his raincoat.*

(8- 6) *Mary was very hungry, but she was trying to lose some weight. She decided to take a diet pill.*

In story (8-5), the normal plan for the goal of getting the newspaper is simply to go outside and get it. However, when it is raining, this will cause one to get rained on, a generally undesirable state. Hence getting the paper is in conflict with staying dry. To resolve this conflict, the ***REPLAN*** meta-plan is used to find the normal plan for just this sort of conflict. That is, using a raincoat is stored as a plan to resolve a goal conflict between having to go outside and not getting wet. ***REPLAN*** looks for a plan applicable to both goals, finds this plan, and applies it.

Similarly, in Story (8-6), there is a conflict between the goal of losing weight and satisfying hunger, as the normal plan for the latter goal involves eating. Again, the ***REPLAN*** meta-plan is used, and the ***USE-NORMAL-PLAN*** strategy applied. The normal plan found that is applicable to both goals is to take a diet pill. This strategy is merely the generalization of the ***USE-NORMAL-PLAN*** planning strategy applied to ***RESOLVE-GOAL-CONFLICT*** meta-goals. Just as many objects are functionally defined by the role they play in ordinary plans, so some objects are functionally defined by the role they play in plans aimed at resolving specific goal conflicts. Thus a diet pill is an object functionally defined by its ability to resolve the conflict between hunger and weight loss; a raincoat is defined by the role it plays in preventing wetness when one must go outside.

Many mundane plans appear to consist of plans for resolving specific types of goal conflicts. For example, putting a lock on one's house is a plan to resolve the conflict between leaving one's home and preventing someone else from entering it in your absence; leaving a message is a plan to resolve the conflict between communicating something to someone and not being able to get in touch with him personally; using a video-recorder to record a show while watching another is a plan to resolve time-based goal conflict specifically involving television shows. Thus a large body of common planning knowledge is organized within the framework of plans aimed at specific goal conflict situations.

At first, one might consider that such plans can simply be stored as plans for one of the goals; for example, using a raincoat is a plan for the preservation goal of not getting wet when it is raining. The difficulty with this organization is that it would not distinguish between such plans and other plans for this goal that are not applicable here. For example, another plan for staying dry when it is raining is to stay indoors. However, this is not useful when one needs to go someplace. To make efficient utilization of knowledge about what to do when it is raining, those plans that are applicable to situations in which other goals are present need to be readily accessible. This is precisely what the organization proposed here does.

Part of the problem here is that since each of these plans is applicable to two goals, these plans could in fact be used in a situation in which only one of the goals is present. For example, one could leave a message for someone when one doesn't have to be anyplace else; one could go outside with a raincoat on when it is not raining. The point is that while these plans will work for a single goal, they are most appropriate for goal conflicts and seem out of place when they are used otherwise.

8.3.1.2 INTELLIGENT USE OF *TRY-ALTERNATIVE-PLAN*

A general planning strategy that is applicable when a plan cannot be made to work is to try another plan for that goal. In the case of resolving goal conflicts, this means that alternative plans for each conflicting goal can be proposed until a set is found that is not in conflict. As noted previously, this might be computationally costly if new plans were proposed blindly. However, there are some intelligent ways of proposing new alternatives that may help keep these costs down.

Consider the following story.

(8- 7) John was going outside to pick up the paper when he noticed it was raining. He looked for his raincoat, but he couldn't find it. He decided to get Fido to fetch the paper for him.

John first thought to walk outside, but then found that this would cause a conflict. Because his normal plan for resolving this conflict failed, John tried proposing other plans, looking for ones that wouldn't entail his getting wet. Since getting the dog to fetch the paper is such a plan, and since John presumably doesn't care if Fido gets wet, this plan is adopted.

The meta-planning strategy used here is called **TRY-ALTERNATIVE-PLAN**. The difference between using this meta-plan and blind generate-and-test strategies is that it implies that some control can be exerted over exactly what is undone and what is looked for as a replacement. That is, the backtracking here need not be chronological, but rather a planning decision related to either goal can be undone.

In addition, when fetching a new plan, it may be possible to specify in the fetch some conditions that the fetched plan may have to meet without actually testing that plan for a conflict. For example, in the case of getting the newspaper when it is raining, the planner can ask its memory for a plan for getting something that does not involve going outside. That is, it can look for a plan for one goal that does not contain an action that led to the original conflict. If the memory mechanism can handle such requests, the planner can retrieve only those plans that do not cause a conflict in the same way that the original plan does.

In order for this to work, **TRY-ALTERNATIVE-PLAN** needs to know what part of a plan contributes to the goal conflict so it can look for a plan without this action. This generally depends on the kind of confict. If the conflict is based on a resource limitation, one should avoid the step that uses the resource. If the conflict is based on mutually exclusive states, we need to avoid the step that results in the exclusive state. If the conflict is based on invoking a presentation goal, one must avoid the step that results in invoking the preservation theme. We can formulate this within the meta-planning framework by defining a meta-plan called **MAKE-ATTRIBUTION** that is used as a subplan of the **TRY-ALTERNATIVE-PLAN** meta-plan. **TRY-ALTERNATIVE-PLAN** first asks **MAKE-ATTRIBUTION** to specify a cause of the problem, and then fetches a new plan without the objectional element in it. This alternative to chronological backtracking is termed *knowledge-directed backtracking*.

TRY-ALTERNATIVE-PLAN can also control how far up the task network to undo a decision. For example, if no alternative plan for a goal can be found, the goal itself can be questioned if it is a subgoal of some other plan. For example, consider the following story.

(8- 8)   *John was going to get the newspaper when he noticed it was raining. He decided to listen to the radio instead.*

Here the entire subtask of getting the newspaper is eliminated. Since this is apparently a subgoal of finding out the news, the alternative plan of listening to the radio can be substituted. **MAKE-ATTRIBUTION** is used here to propose a plan that does not involve an unwanted step. The difference between this and the previous case is that here a plan to which a conflicting goal is instrumental is replanned.

8.3.2 *CHANGE-CIRCUMSTANCE*

In addition to the **REPLAN** meta-plan, the other general goal conflict resolution strategy is to change the circumstance that contributes to the conflict. This is actually more general than **REPLAN**, because it may be applicable to mutually exclusive states conflicts where the exclusive states are the goals themselves, whereas **REPLAN** required the conflict to be plan-based.

CHANGE-CIRCUMSTANCE can resolve a goal conflict by altering a state of the world that is responsible for the goals conflicting with one another. Once this has been achieved, the original set of plans may be used without encountering the original problem. For example, consider the following stories:

(8- 9) *John had a meeting with his boss in the morning, but he was feeling ill and wanted to stay in bed. He decided to call his boss and try to postpone the meeting until he felt better.* .

(8-10) *John wanted to live in San Francisco, but he also wanted to live near Mary, and she lived in New York. John tried to persuade Mary to move to San Francisco with him.*

In story (8-9), John's conflict is caused by his plan to attend the meeting and his plan to stay home and rest. These plans conflict because of the time constraints on John's meeting, which force the plans to overlap; the plans require John to be in two places at once, so they cannot be executed simultaneously. If the time constraint on attending the meeting were relaxed, the conflict would cease to exist. Thus, rather than alter his plans, John can seek to change the circumstances that cause his plans to conflict by attempting to remove the time constraint that is a cause of the difficulty.

In story (8-10), the conflict is between living in San Francisco and being near Mary, who is in New York. The basis for this exclusion involves the location of San Francisco and that of Mary. However, if one of these locations were changed so that the distance between them were reduced, the one state would no longer exclude the other. Thus John can attempt to change Mary's location, while still maintaining his original goals.

To decide what circumstance to change, a planner once again needs to analyze the cause of the conflict. Thus **CHANGE-CIRCUMSTANCE** first requires the use of **MAKE-ATTRIBUTION** to propose a candidate for alteration. As was the case for **REPLAN**, **MAKE-ATTRIBUTION** requires access to knowledge about the class of negative interactions discussed in the previous chapter. This knowledge is needed here in order to find a particular circumstance with which to meddle. A description of how this knowledge is used to isolate a candidate for consideration follows.

8.3.2.1 *CHANGE-CIRCUMSTANCE* FOR RESOURCE SHORTAGES

If the conflict is caused by a shortage of a resource, the lack of that resource can be blamed for the conflict. The exact way of framing the problem depends on the class of resource. We will consider conflicts based on time and those caused by consumable objects.

Time-based conflicts are caused by time constraints and by the inability to execute two plans at once. Thus the strategy of **CHANGE-CIRCUMSTANCE** applied here amounts to one of the following:

1. *Remove a deadline*
2. *Change the timing of an external event*
3. *Abandon a background goal*
4. *Increase an ability*
5. *Increase the capacity of a functional object*

These alternatives are illustrated by the following stories.

(8-11)   *John wanted to talk to Mary, but her train left in five minutes. John tried to get the conductor to delay the departure.*

(8-12)   *John didn't have enough time both to watch the football game and study for his exam. He decided to watch the game and stay up all night and study.*

(8-13)   *John had too much reading between his English class and his Political Science course. He decided to enroll in a speed reading program.*

(8-14)   *John was trying to cook two dishes on his one-burner camping stove. He walked over to a neighboring camper and asked if he could borrow his Coleman.*

All these examples involve goal conflicts based on time. Story (8-11) involves an attempt to remove a time constraint so that the plans selected no longer conflict. In story (8-12), the background goal of sleep is normally presumed to be scheduled, but this may be given up as a way of obtaining more time. In story (8-13), a limitation on abilities is involved as well; thus the additional option of trying to enhance that ability may be attempted. Story (8-14) involves a limitation on the capacity of a functional object; the enhancement of this capacity is thus a viable resolution.

When a consumable object is the cause of the conflict, the conflict can be eliminated by obtaining more of the consumable.

8.3.2.2   *CHANGE-CIRCUMSTANCE* **FOR MUTUALLY EXCLUSIVE STATES**

Conflicts based on mutually exclusive states are usually based on some premise in addition to the particular state in conflict. For example, conflicts based on social exclusion require a cultural prohibition; therefore one may try to undo the prohibition, ignore it and take the consequences, or try to change one's culture, as the following stories demonstrate.

(8-15)   *John wanted to marry Mary; he also wanted to marry Sue.*
         (a) He decided to become a Muslim and move to Saudi Arabia.
         (b) He decided to go ahead and risk being prosecuted for bigamy.
         (c) He decided to start a campaign to make bigamy acceptable.

Even when the exclusion is logical, the rules of inference may draw on other facts about the world. In the case of story (8-10), for example, the goals are exclusive because a person cannot be at two places at once; however this requires that the location of the two places be different. Thus this problem can be resolved by changing one of the locations to be more convenient.

8.3.2.3   *CHANGE-CIRCUMSTANCE* **FOR PRESERVATION GOAL-BASED CONFLICTS**

CHANGE-CIRCUMSTANCE and *MAKE-ATTRIBUTION* are particularly useful for resolving this kind of conflict. For example, consider the following stories.

(8-16)   *John wanted to spend the day on the beach, but he thought his boss would fire him. He decided to call in sick.*

(8-17)   *John wanted to get the newspaper, but it was raining. He held an old piece of newspaper over his head and went outside.*

(8-18)   *John wanted to save Mary from the dragon, but he was a coward. He decided to get drunk and make a mad charge.*

As in the previous cases, additional factors are presumed to cause the conflict. In story (8-16), the presumption is that the boss would get angry at John and fire him if he knew the actual reason for John's absence. However, if a false reason is substituted, John's action will not lead to the undesirable result. Similarly, in story (8-17), being in the rain causes objects to get wet; if something is between the rain and the object, this will not happen. In story (8-18), experiencing fear prevents John from rescuing Mary, but being drunk changes the circumstances so that his actions are not likely to have this effect.

In all of these case, the finer details of the conflict are examined, and some piece of it challenged. *MAKE-ATTRIBUTION* needs to determine which component is a good candidate for undoing. First a relatively easy condition may be tackled, and if that fails to work, progressively harder ones may be tried. This of course requires knowledge about the probable difficulty of goals; but this is the same knowledge one would need in tasks in which difficulty assessments must be made, such as selection among several possible plans for some goal.

Note that some of the plans produced this way may resemble normal plans for a goal conflict. For example, putting a newspaper over one's head to go outside is reminiscent of using an umbrella. This is because even canned plans are motivated by some underlying considerations. In particular, the *REPLAN* and *CHANGE-CIRCUMSTANCE* meta-plans explain how a set of plans can be altered to avoid a conflict. Thus the normal plans for a goal conflict are just institutionalized versions of plans based on these general considerations.

8.4   GOAL ABANDONMENT

When attempts to resolve a goal conflict are unsuccessful, a planner must make a decision about what should be salvaged from this situation. The choices here involve abandoning some of the goals completely and pursuing some select subset, or fulfilling some of the goals only to a degree. I consider the latter alternative (partial goal fulfillment) to be a form of goal abandonment rather than conflict resolution because the strategy does not result in the fulfillment of the original set of goals.

In terms of meta-planning, goal abandonment situations can be described as follows. The inability to achieve a *RESOLVE-GOAL-CONFLICT* meta-goal results in the planner having this failed meta-goal on his hands (or, more precisely, in his representational space). Having a failed *RESOLVE-GOAL-CONFLICT* meta-goal is a condition that triggers the meta-theme **MAXIMIZE THE VALUE OF THE GOALS ACHIEVED**. The triggering condition causes this meta-theme to invoke a new meta-goal, called ***CHOOSE-MOST-VALUABLE-SCENARIO***. This goal is satisfied when the relative worth of various achievable subsets of the conflicting goals is assessed, and the subset offering the greatest potential yield is determined.

To achieve this meta-goal, I postulate a ***SIMULATE-AND-SELECT*** meta-plan. This plan proposes various combinations of goals to try and computes the worth of each combination. The most valuable set of goals is returned as the scenario most worth pursuing.

8.4.1 The *SIMULATE-AND-SELECT* Meta-plan

The ***SIMULATE-AND-SELECT*** meta-plan has a rich structure. To begin with, it makes a number of presumptions about evaluating the cost and worth of goals and of comparing them to one another. These are general issues discussed in Chapter 4. For the purposes at hand, I will not dwell on exactly how the evaluation is done. This is partly because the details of how to do this are not completely clear, but more so because they are not crucial for the upcoming discussion. Recall that I presume that values can be attributed to individual states in isolation *ceteris paribus*, and that the value of a set can be computed from its parts. This does not presume that the computation is simple; indeed, it may involve the consultation of large amounts of world knowledge. However, I do assume that all values can be made commeasurable.

The ***SIMULATE-AND-SELECT*** meta-plan has two distinct options. The first is quite straightforward. It simply involves constructing maximal achievable (i.e., nonconflicting) subsets from among the conflicting goals, and evaluating the net worth of each subset. Since we are generally dealing with two goals in a conflict, this means just evaluating the worth of one goal and comparing it to the value of the other. Thus, if having the newspaper is deemed more valuable than getting wet, the planner walks outside to get the newspaper and allows himself to get soaked. Alternatively, a reader trying to understand someone else's behavior would use knowledge about this meta-plan to make inferences about their value system. If a reader observes John risking getting wet to get his morning paper, the reader concludes that having his paper is worth more to him than avoiding getting wet.

Sometimes goal abandonment operates in a sort of disguise. Consider the following stories.

(8-19)   *John wanted to see the football game, but his wife said she would divorce him if he watched one more game. John settled for watching the tennis match together with his wife.*

(8-20)   *John wanted to live in San Francisco, but he also wanted to live near Mary, and she lived in New York. John decided he could probably find another girlfriend in San Francisco.*

In story (8-19), John must resolve a conflict between his goal of watching the football game and preserving his marriage. On the surface, it appears as if John modifies the goal of watching the football game to watching tennis instead, an activity to which John's wife apparently does not object. Similarly, in story (8-20), John abandons his goal of maintaining his relationship with Mary, and appears to substitute it with the goal of having a similar relationship with somebody else.

Schank and Abelson (1977) describe such situations as instances of *goal substitution*. According to them, goal substitution is a strategy applicable whenever a goal is blocked. They state the rule that "following blockage, the maximum feasible number of valued characteristics of the goal object should be preserved." As they point out, goals can be "stacked" within a hierarchy of many levels. For example, wanting to watch the Giants can be an instance of wanting to watch a football game, which in turn is an instance of wanting to watch a sporting event, and so on. If a goal is to be substituted, it is desirable to replace it with a goal occupying as similar a place in the hierarchy as the goal it is replacing. So watching the Jets is likely to be a better substitution for watching the Giants than is watching tennis, which is in turn a better substitute than mowing the lawn.

However, I offer an analysis that is somewhat at odds with theirs. The main problem with Schank and Abelson's formulation is based on a subtle distinction. To see this distinction, consider the question of *why* one goal may be substituted for another. That is, how is it possible that a "similar" goal can be substituted for the original goal? If a goal is truly something that a planner wants to achieve, why should some other, different state do as well? The answer that Schank and Abelson provide is that the original goal is really just an instantiation of a more general goal; therefore another instantiation will do.

The problem here is that we are forced to conclude that the original goal was not a goal at all, but merely a plan for achieving some real goal. This is clearly the case some of the time, as the following story illustrates.

(8-21) *John needed a pen to sign a letter. When he couldn't find his own, he asked Bill if he could borrow his.*

In this example, John at one point seems to have the goal of possessing his pen. When this goal fails, he replaces it with the goal of possessing Bill's pen. On the surface, one goal appears to be substituted by another, similar goal. However, strictly speaking, it is unlikely that John really had the goal of possessing his pen; most likely, his goal was "possess some pen" or possibly, "possess a writing implement." But such a goal is too abstract to be achieved directly. While this goal is not specific to the particular writing implement selected, the real world has only individual objects. At some point, one such object must be designated in order for a plan to be executed. That is, in order to have any pen, a planner must eventually plan to obtain one particular pen.

Because this sort of narrowing down is really part of the planning process rather than part of a planner's goal structure, I refer to it as *plan specification*. Specifically I postulate a **PLAN-SPECIFICATION** meta-plan that makes a plan work by supplanting generic descriptions with descriptions of more specific entities. (This is in contrast to *goal specification,* a term used by Schank and Abelson to make the conditions of a goal more elaborate. The effects of these two processes is quite different. Plan specification enables the fulfillment of a goal by producing a plan more amenable to execution. Goal specification makes fulfillment of a goal more difficult by posing additional constraints that a state must meet in order to constitute fulfillment of that goal.)

John wanting his pen in story (8-21) is an instance of plan specification. His goal is to have a writing implement, and as a way of achieving this goal he used the **PLAN-SPECIFICATION** meta-plan to produce the plan of obtaining his particular pen. However, because this plan fails, the planner replans by respecifying another instance of the generic class of object which he is seeking.

Thus the situation in story (8-21) obeys Schank and Abelson's hierarchy rules, but it is unrelated to goal substitution; it merely supplants one plan with another and it is therefore an instance of replanning for a goal. For a real goal substitution to occur, an actual goal rather than a plan-specified instance of a goal must be substituted. Otherwise this situation is no different than substituting one plan for another when an attempt to execute that plan fails.

Most of Schank and Abelson's candidates for goal substitution are instances of replanning. For example, consider that goal of "enjoy eating at a Chinese restaurant." Schank and Abelson suggest that this is "dominated" by the goal "enjoy eating good food," and therefore, if it fails, eating at a French restaurant may be substituted as it preserves these salient features. But in fact, these features are not a property of this goal at all. To see this, note that the goal dominating this one may just have easily been "partake in the Chinese New Year celebration." Now if eating at a Chinese restaurant were blocked, a reasonable substitute might be "watch the Chinese New Year parade." However, "enjoy eating at a French restaurant" would fail utterly. The explanation for this difference is that in both cases, eating at a Chinese restaurant is not a goal, but rather a plan for another goal.

Of course, "enjoy eating at a Chinese restaurant" could be an actual goal, but in that case, it would be unsubstitutable. This being a real goal would be most unusual, but in general, such goals do exist. For example, the goal "treat my wife to dinner for her birthday" will hardly be amenable to substitution by replacing my wife with my son, or with her twin sister. And if I really wanted to take her out to dinner, buying her a ring will just not do.

According to the analysis offered here, goal substitution is just not possible. The semantics of what it means to be a goal are such that if one were substitutable, our original specification must have been incorrect in the first place. If I said my goal were "treat my wife to dinner for her birthday," but treating her to a fancy lunch were an acceptable substitute, I must have meant that my original goal was really "treat wife to fancy meal," and the "treat her to dinner" merely a plan.

However, one problem still remains. If I desire to treat my wife to dinner and this goal fails, buying her a ring still seems like an appropriate substitution. The reason for this is that when a planner has a goal such as taking one's spouse to dinner, he often has other related goals as well. For example, he is likely to have the goal ''enjoy a good meal'' and ''buy wife a present'' in addition to the particular desire to take her to dinner. While these goals are in principle unrelated, it happens to be the case that the plan for the latter one is in fact equivalent to the achievement of the other two. That is, in addition to being a goal in its own right, taking one's spouse to dinner is a plan for enjoying a good meal and for buying her a present. Rather than an instance of goal substitution, replacing ''take wife to dinner'' with ''buy her a ring'' is actually an abandonment of this goal and of ''enjoy good meal,'' and a respecification of the ''buy wife a present'' goal with the plan ''buy wife a ring'' instead of ''take wife to dinner.''

In sum, goal substitution does not exist. Either we have a case of respecification, in which the original ''goal'' was actually a plan, or we have an instance of goal abandonment, in which one of the goals abandoned also happens to be equivalent to a plan for another goal, which is in turn respecified to some new plan.

As an example, in story (8-1), suppose we assume John's goal were really to watch the football game. In this case, he actually abandons this goal completely. However, he might have another goal, ''enjoy leisure activity'' for which watching the football game is a plan. Thus watching tennis is a new plan specification for this goal, and the original goal that conflicted with preserving his marriage is given up entirely.

This notion of goal abandonment is sufficient to handle situations like (8-19) and (8-20), once we realize that a number of goals are likely to be active here at once. Of course, making such a realization requires knowledge about the normal goal structures people are likely to have. In the case of story understanding, for example, if we are told that a planner desires such and such a state, we use our knowledge of normalcy to infer what the goal really is. Unusually specific or general goals must be described as such explicitly to overcome this default inference. Thus ''John wanted to go to New York'' is interpreted as the goal ''John wanted to be in New York,'' as going in itself is not normally desirable; if we hear ''John wanted a hamburger,'' we interpret this as ''John wanted some generic hamburger,'' as individual hamburgers are rarely distinguished by one's goals. This tendency toward normalcy is why story (8-20) seems somewhat unusual. One is supposed to highly value the particular individual involved in a relationship, thus realizing that the goal here is actually more abstract comes as somewhat of a surprise.

8.4.2 Partial Goal Fulfillment

Goal abandonment can account for a number of diverse, complicated situations. However, there is another set of situations with which we cannot yet cope. Consider once again the example of fetching the newspaper in from the rain, in which the original goals are to get the newspaper and to remain dry. Rather than abandon either goal completely, a reasonable alternative is to try to reduce the degree to which one gets wet as much as possible. A plan for remaining as dry as possible while moving through the rain is to run as fast as one can. This plan satisfies one goal entirely and another goal to a degree. The total value of this scenario is likely to be greater than the value of staying dry but not getting the paper. Since the other abandonment possibility (getting the paper but getting soaked), is clearly worse than this (i.e., getting the paper but getting less soaked), the scenario involving partial fulfillment is likely to be adopted.

Partial goal fulfillment is a general principle that is applicable to all goals that involve scalar values. If one wants not to be hungry, being less hungry is not as good as not being hungry at all, but it is better than not being less hungry. That is, it is implicit in what it means to be a goal that states closer to the goal, have a value less than the goal, but greater than those further from the goal.

In the cases where this does not appear to hold, it is usually because the actual goal structure has been incorrectly identified. For example, if it were raining acid rain whose very touch were deadly, getting just a little wet would not be better than getting very wet. But this is because the real goal in this situation is not "don't get wet," but "don't get killed." Not getting wet is simply a plan for this goal when it is raining acid rain. Achieving the plan to a degree does not fulfill the goal at all and is thus not a very good plan. In the previous case, the goal is not such a binary one, so partial fulfillment is possible.

Partial goal fulfillment provides the *SIMULATE-AND-SELECT* meta-plan with a complicated option. In addition to strict abandonment scenarios, it now also has the possibility of proposing options in which the partial fulfillment of one goal enables the (possibly partial) fulfillment of the other. The process that proposes this partial fulfillment scenario is as follows: *MAKE-ATTRIBUTION* determines that the problem with the "stay dry" goal is that it requires not going outside. Thus a partial version of this goal is sought that does not involve this condition. In the case of not getting wet, the "stay as dry as possible" alternative is postulated because this does not require going outside. This scenario is hypothesized and evaluated along with the strict abandonment options, and the one with the highest value is chosen.

8.4.3 Plausibility Evaluation

So far, I have been assuming that the planner has absolute certainty about each scenario that is envisioned. However, a planner may believe that different scenarios will fulfill his various goals with different degrees of certainty. Since the degree of expectation of success affects the overall value of the scenario, the planner must take these factors into account in selecting an option.

For example, if the planner believes that some scenario offers a very small chance of fulfilling a very important goal, but a competing scenario offers a larger chance of fulfilling a less important goal, then these likelihoods must be considered in determining which scenario is to be preferred. Thus crossing the street may be in conflict with not getting hit by a car, and the value of preserving one's life is apt to be greater than the ultimate value of the goal underlying crossing the street. However, the perceived likelihood of such an occurrence is usually so small as to undermine the superior value of that goal from influencing one's decision.

Once the probability of success enters into consideration, the situations I have been calling goal conflicts are actually often only plausible conflicts. That is, all the goal conflict detection and reasoning apparatus that has been discussed so far may be called into play when the planner expects that pursuing one goal may impede the fulfillment of another, but in which the interference itself may be only probabilistic.

Fortunately these considerations can be accommodated without serious alterations to the planning structures proposed thus far if we assume that the planner can attach plausibility judgments to anticipated events and propagate these judgments to the derived scenarios. Then the descriptions of situations used by the Goal Detector to spot goal conflicts can contain the degree of plausibility of the goal as well. For example, the planner might have a description denoting that walking down a dark alley alone at night conflicts to some particular degree with preserving one's money. Upon considering such an action, this possible conflict will be inferred, just as would a certain conflict. Then the relative values and likelihoods of fulfillments of the goals could be considered to determine the appropriate course of action.

To propagate plausibility judgments, the planner needs to be able to access the probability that a plan will succeed if all its preconditions are fulfilled; then the interaction wth the other plans amounts to accessing the probability that those preconditions will be met. A goal conflict, then, is a situation in which pursuing one plan lowers the probability of the preconditions for some other plan being met.

In situations in which the likelihood and values of the goals involved favor the same goal, selecting the most productive scenario is unproblematic. However, in those situations in which the values and expected achievement of goals are inversely related, a way of comparing these quantities is needed. However, the computation of the expected value of the plan of action does not appear to be something that people carry out in a principled way. That is, these situations are those in which it is notoriously difficult for people to come to a decision. Possibly, rather than a principled means of computing expected value, a set of heuristics is used. My theory need not commit itself on this point, however. We need only assume that the value of a scenario computed by **SIMULATE-AND-SELECT** takes into account the relative likelihood of success in addition to the value of one's goal. The execution of this meta-plan may spawn subplans like consulting an expert if a difficult decision is involved. Like any other plan, the **SIMULATE-AND-SELECT** plan may simply fail altogether, leaving the planner in a quandary as to which action to take.

8.4.4 An Example

As many of the situations just described are complicated by the presence of a number of goals all involving the same plan, it is instructive to look at one such situation in some detail. One plan I might have for eating lunch is to go to the Three C's with Lotfi and order a crepe. The goal structure behind this seemingly simple plan is actually quite rich. First, this plan seeks to satisfy several goals:

1. Satisfy my hunger.
2. Enjoy eating.
3. Get back to the office quickly.
4. Enjoy company.
5. Not spending much money.

If in fact these are precisely my goals, the plan I chose is only one of a number of alternatives that might work just as well. For example, I could conceivably go to another restaurant that is equidistant and which serves just as good food, or I might try another companion if the one specified in this plan were not available. These variations would fulfill the actual goal just as well and thus constitute instances of respecification rather than goal substitution.

On the other hand, if no restaurant near my office were opened, I might have to settle for the partial fulfillment of a goal, namely, I would attempt to get back as little late as possible. Or if the only good restaurant nearby served very small portions, I would have a goal conflict between "satisfy hunger" and "enjoy good food." This conflict might be resolved once again by settling for partial fulfillment, achieving "'satisfy hunger' as much as possible" rather than "satisfy hunger."

Alternatively, my original goal structure could have been somewhat different. For example, I might have had an urge for a Three C's crepe, in which case going to another good restaurant would have to be viewed as goal abandonment. Or I might have had some particular reason to talk with Lotfi, so choosing another co-diner would not be acceptable. It is unlikely, however, that I would have had only very general original goals like "enjoy any activity" and "satisfy some urge," so that when I could find no restaurant opened nearby, I would be just as happy to go watch a movie with a friend. Of course, I might actually end up doing so in this situation. But such an action would then have to be interpreted as abandoning a number of my original goals rather than as finding a different way of achieving them.

8.5 HAVING THE CONFLICT RESOLVED FOR YOU

The goal conflicts in the previous sections required some action by the planner to either reach a resolution or choose the least of several evils. However, a planner or an understander must be prepared to cope with another set of possibilities.

Sometimes a goal conflict can be resolved by a series of events that are unrelated to the action of the planner. For example, consider the following stories.

(8-22)   John wanted to watch the football game, but he had a paper due the next day. Then the teacher postponed the assignment for a week.

(8-23)   John enjoyed smoking marijuana, but he was paranoid about getting busted. Then one day the city council voted to legalize drugs.

Each case describes a rather standard goal conflict. Moreover, the goal conflicts are resolved in accordance with essentially the same principles as were given in the previous sections. However, in these cases, the events resolving the conflict occur spontaneously with respect to the planner.

In the theory of meta-planning, such an occurrence may be treated simply as a spontaneous change in the possibility of fulfilling a meta-goal. That is, when a planner has any goal, the state at which this goal is aimed could come into existence by the act of another planner or by natural circumstances. For example, if a planner desired to have a house on the beach, he might find one day that he inherited one. This planner, or an understander observing these events, would have to realize that the goal of obtaining a beach house should no longer be pursued, even though no plan for achieving it has been executed successfully. That is, the planner or an understander must have the ability to relate observed events to the planner's goals.

In the case of a goal conflict, a meta-goal of resolving the goal conflict is present. The spontaneous goal conflict resolutions reached in the preceding examples are simply a spontaneous fulfillment of this meta-goal. For example, when the teacher postpones the deadline in story (8-22), this spontaneously fulfills the planner's **RESOLVE-GOAL-CONFLICT** meta-goal in exactly the same way that the planner's relative bequeathing him a beach house fulfills the goal of owning a beach house. Namely, a situation amounting to the conditions of successful execution of some plan for the goal comes into existence. For the goal of owning a beach house, the transfer of ownership normally brought about by the plan of buying the beach house occurs, while in the case of resolving the goal conflict, a change in the availability of a resource normally brought about by a **CHANGE-CIRCUMSTANCE** meta-plan occurs spontaneously.

The point of this correspondence is that no additional mechanism is required to monitor spontaneous goal conflict resolutions other than that already required to monitor the spontaneous fulfillment of an ordinary goal. Since this capability must be present to understand a situation in which ordinary goals are fulfilled, it can be applied to the detection of spontaneous resolution without additional cost. This case is an instance of a typical benefit of the meta-planning approach—a mechanism required for ordinary planning situations can be applied the more complicated case of goal interaction without postulating additional mechanisms specifically for this task.

Tracking the changes in the possibility of achieving a goal is actually more general than just looking for its spontaneous fulfillment. For example, rather than bring about a goal state, an event may make the fulfillment of a goal more difficult to achieve. For example, if a planner wanted to own a particular beach house, but the house were destroyed in a fire, the achievement of this goal is impossible. The planner's appropriate course of behavior is to abandon this goal (the general planning principle involved here is the meta-theme **AVOID IMPOSSIBLE GOALS**). In the case of goal conflicts, this sort of information is also useful. For example, if the goal of having this particular beach house were in conflict with, say, taking a world tour, the beach house burning to the ground would eliminate the conflict just as surely as inheriting it would. We need only require that the planner recompute all the relationships that a goal formerly entered into when that goal is abandoned. It will be abandoned by the principle just described, and this recomputation will show that the former goal conflict now fails to exist.

8.6 SUMMARY

A number of situations are based on goal conflicts. A goal conflict may cause a planner to fail to achieve a goal; it may cause a planner to try to resolve the conflict; or the conflict may be resolved by an incidental action. To deal with these situations, a reader or a planner must be able to detect goal conflicts and use knowledge about the nature of goal conflicts to determine the appropriate behavior.

A number of strategies are available to a planner experiencing this sort of difficulty. The planner may try to resolve the problem by replanning, or it may try to change the circumstances that caused the goals to give rise to the problem in the first place. This failing, the planner may try to abandon one or more goals in order to permit the achievement of some of the others. One type of abandonment scenario involves partial achievement of the planners goals as a possible way of achieving the most desirable overall effect.

9

Reasoning About Goal Competition

9.1 INTRODUCTION

Thus far we have considered how a planner might deal with the problems that result from an adverse interaction of its own goals. Problems may also arise from the interaction of one's goals with the goals of another planner. In these goal competition situations, a planner may have to take into account the intentions and actions of other planners in order to fulfill his goal. Similarly, an understander may have to use knowledge about dealing with adversaries to explain the actions of a character whose goal competes with someone else's.

Previously, I defined several classes of goal competition and described how they could be detected by a planner or an understander. This chapter examines the situations that may develop from the existence of goal competition. Although a resemblance between the kinds of goal conflict and goal competition has been noted, reasoning about the situations to which they give rise differs considerably. In fact, the similarities in classification turn out to be rather superficial in this regard.

The reason for this is that while goal conflict and goal competition are based on almost identical logical structures, they play very different roles with respect to the semantics of goals and, thereby, to planning and understanding. The notion of how to behave in the presence of a goal conflict is basic to what it means to be a goal. That is, to understand what goals are and how planners possessing them should act requires knowledge about goal conflicts per se. For example, we may interpret someone's behavior as being rational even if he abandons an achievable goal, as long as we recognize that this goal is in conflict with some other, more important goal. This is knowledge about what goals one should favor in the event of a conflict and it cannot be derived from considerations about individual goals. Thus an understanding of goal conflicts is necessary for the most basic understanding of the nature of goals.

Goal competition, on the other hand, does not occupy such a privileged position. The presence of competition makes it more difficult to achieve a given goal, but it does not help to define what it means for something to be a goal. Rather, the factors underlying goal competition ground out on more basic principles. For example, suppose someone in a goal competition situation decides to abandon a goal because that person is afraid of hurting the competitor's feeings. In my model, I would state that the planner had another goal of not hurting this other individual, that this goal *conflicted* with the original goal, and that the planner opted for abandoning the original goal as the way of maximizing the value of the goals achieved. However, this is a principle related to goal conflict, rather than a principle of competition in its own right, that forms the basis for the decision.

Another way of saying this is that planners are motivated by their own goal structure; they are affected by other planner's goals only insofar as those goals affect their own. The existence of a competing goal merely informs the planner of potential problems it may have in achieving its goal, but it does not in itself form a part of the planner's goal structure.

This difference has a number of consequences that distinguish reasoning about goal competition from reasoning about goal conflict. First, most of the knowledge about competition is in the form of plans about how to deal with competition, whereas knowledge about conflict is also concerned with which goals a planner should select. Thus goal conflict has a richer meta-planning structure, because it involves multiple goals of the same planner, whereas goal competition considerations are simply strategies for assuring the fulfillment of a goal. Second, while the strategies for dealing with goal conflict are ordered (e.g., it is appropriate to try to resolve a conflict before deciding to abandon a goal), there does not appear to be such an ordering on the methods for dealing with goal competition. That is, the appropriateness of a plan is determined by planning principles that do not select out particular competition strategies as preferable on their own merits.

9.2 SITUATIONS THAT RESULT FROM GOAL COMPETITION

Consider the following goal competition stories.

(9- 1) *The western nations all strove for control of China. They eventually reached a compromise and divided it up into spheres of influence.*

(9- 2) *John wanted to play golf, but Mary thought he should mow the lawn. John decided to hire a kid to mow the lawn for him.*

(9- 3) *John and Bill both wanted to win the race. They each ran as hard as they could.*

(9- 4) *John and Bill both wanted to win the race. Before the race, John slipped Bill a mickey.*

(9- 5) *John and Bill were rivals for Mary's hand in marriage. One day, John fell in love with another woman.*

As these examples suggest, there are a number of alternatives that a planner may select when faced with a goal competition situation. These categories are mostly strategies a planner may use to prevent a competitive situation from interfering with the fulfillment of its goal. The following categories partition the situations to which goal competition can give rise:

1. Goal Competition Resolution—In these situations, one or both of the characters with competing goals makes an effort to avoid competing with one another. Stories (9-1) and (9-2) are both instances of this category. In (9-2) the efforts involve only a single planner; in (9-1) both parties modify their plans to eliminate competition.

2. Competitive Plan Execution—Rather than eliminate the competition, a planner may alter its plans to directly take into account the competitive nature of one's goal. Stories (9-3) and (9-4) are instances of competitive plan execution. In (9-3) one merely tries to outdo the other; in (9-4) one planner takes action to try to undermine his opponent's efforts.

3. Spontaneous Competition Removal—As is the case for goal conflict, competition may be spontaneously eliminated by no act of the planner involved. This is the case in story (9-5), in which John's interference with Bill's goal is fortuitously eliminated. Of course, this situation is not a strategy, but merely a state of affairs of which a planner or an understander must be aware to recognize an appropriate course of action.

The motivation for the existence of these categories, as well as for selecting one or the other as a strategy, is derived from the meta-planning principles already introduced rather than from any principles specific to goal competition. For example, suppose a planner decides to replan so as to avoid competition. He may do so because he believes that the plan leading to competition will be harder to execute than one that does not involve competition. If so, the motivation is derived from the **DON'T WASTE RESOURCES** meta-theme. On the other hand, he may avoid competition simply because he finds it distasteful. In this case, his original plan conflicts with a goal of avoiding competition, and the replanning is really a means for goal conflict resolution.

The remainder of this chapter discusses each of these goal competition situations in detail.

9.3 GOAL COMPETITION RESOLUTION

One or both of the planners involved in a goal competition situation may seek to circumvent the competitive nature of their plans. Resolution of the competition may be desirable on the part of a planner for a variety of reasons:

1. Competition can lead to goal conflict—Sometimes the competitive nature of a plan will end up causing a conflict for its planner. Then all the principles involving goal conflict are brought into play. These motivate resolving the competition as well as suggest methods for doing so. For example, suppose John wants to run away with Bill's wife, but he realizes that he may have to kill Bill to do so. Killing Bill may be undesirable for a number of reasons, so John's competitive plan results in a goal conflict. Now all the goal conflict strategies are applicable. For example, *REPLAN* or *CHANGE-CIRCUMSTANCE* may be used together with *MAKE-ATTRIBUTION* to try to find a way of being with Bill's wife that does not cause this particular problem to arise.

Conflict may also arise simply because the planner finds competition itself distasteful or fears undesirable consequences, such as generating enmity. In any case, the conflict becomes apparent to the planner in the simulation of his plan, just as other forms of goal conflict are detected. However, in addition to the standard plans for conflict resolution, some specific options (to be discussed later) are available in the case of goal competition.

2. Competition may be costly—The planner may judge the competitive plan to be too costly compared to other plans that may be available. For example, a competitive plan may require the planner to expend energy struggling with an adversary, while a noncompetitive plan may be less strenuous. In this case, the **DON'T WASTE RESOURCES** meta-theme would set up a meta-goal of selecting a less costly alternative.

3. Competition may reduce chances of success—In addition to competition making it costly to fulfill a goal, and possibly jeopardizing other goals, resolution of the competition may also decrease the chances of fulfilling the original goal. That is, when faced with a formidable competitor, the chance that a plan will succeed will be reduced, motivating the selection of an alternative plan.

None of these reasons is necessarily compelling in any particular situation. For example, it is possible that a particular planner finds competition itself appealing. For this planner, a competitive plan would constitute a goal overlap rather than goal conflict situation, and it is likely to be chosen over a noncompetitive plan, all other things being equal. Alternatively, a plan that is competitive may still be less costly than some other, noncompetitive plan, and thus it may be selected on that basis.

However, once a planner has decided to eliminate a plan because it entails competition, the following strategies are available:

1. Independent Plan Alteration—A planner unilaterally modifies its plan to eliminate its competitive nature.

2. Induced Alteration—One planner may persuade another to modify a competitive plan.

9.3.1 Independent Plan Alteration

A planner wishing to produce a noncompetitive alternative to its current plan may do so on its own simply by using the *REPLAN* and *CHANGE-CIRCUMSTANCE* meta-plans, together with the *MAKE-ATTRIBUTION* subplan. That is, the planner can use *MAKE-ATTRIBUTION* to determine the aspects of the plan that cause the competition to result. Then the planner can either try to find another plan that does not have these features (*REPLAN*), or try to change the conditions that cause these features to be problematic (*CHANGE-CIRCUMSTANCE*).

Consider the following story.

(9- 6)   John was planning to cross through the jungle, but when he learned it was inhabited by dangerous headhunters, he decided to take the long way around.

Here the original plan gives rise to a dangerously competitive situation: crossing the jungle is likely to cause the headhunters to attack John, causing him to have a preservation goal. He therefore decides on an alternative plan that will not cause the dangerous situation to arise. Note that the planning in this example is done strictly in terms of goal conflict—no special knowledge of goal competition per se is needed. One only has to realize that the headhunters are likely to attack. (From the perspective of planning in this example, they might as well have been inanimate dangers.)

Thus far, we have not really needed goal competition as a category, as the situations we have considered can be handled strictly by goal conflict strategies. However, some planning knowledge about goal competition finds its way into the plans used to deal with goal conflicts arising from the anticipated competing goal of other planners. For example, one application of *CHANGE-CIRCUMSTANCE* is to reduce the cause of the competition. Thus, if the competition is caused by the shortage of some resource, *CHANGE-CIRCUMSTANCE* may recommending getting more of that resource and then proceeding with the original plan. Of course, knowledge of how goals can compete would be needed to make such an inference.

A broad class of scenarios involving *CHANGE-CIRCUMSTANCE* is termed "anticipated goal competition situations." In general, the strategy here is to execute a plan in such a way as not to cause one's opponent to have a competing goal.

For example, story (9-6) contains an anticipated goal competition situation, as John anticipated that his plan would invoke a competitive goal in some other planner. While he used a conflict resolution strategy here, in general, knowledge specific to goal competition is needed to apply *CHANGE-CIRCUMSTANCE*. Consider the following stories.

(9- 7)   *John was planning to cross through the jungle, but then he learned it was inhabited by dangerous headhunters.*
(a) He decided to go through the jungle at night.
(b) He crossed the jungle so fast that the natives never spotted him.
(c) He created a fire and crossed the jungle while the natives were in panic.
(d) He disguised himself as an animal and made it across unnoticed.
(e) He fooled the natives into thinking he was bringing them gifts, and they let him pass.

These examples are all instances of avoiding invoking a theme. That is, the structure of anticipated goal competition situations involves performing an event the perception of which invokes some theme in another planner, which in turn causes that planner to have a competing goal. One way to avoid competition is therefore to prevent such a perception from occurring in the first place. The planner can try to accomplish this in a number of ways: by preventing the perception of the action altogether, by performing the action in such a way that it will be perceived differently, or by supplying his potential opponent with a false but plausible motivation for the action.

Thus we have a class of strategies within *CHANGE-CIRCUMSTANCES* for avoiding invoking a theme. These strategies are all motivated by the structure of the situation that invokes that theme. In general, the action resulting from one's plan will be perceived by one's opponent; then the opponent will infer the planner's intentions, recognize their consequences, and some theme will then be invoked. This structure is illustrated in Fig. 9.1.

Note in Fig. 9.1 that the Opponent's goal G2 is shown to compete with some goal of the Planner, called Gn. This may or may not be the same as the Planner's original goal. For example, in the case of John trying to cross the jungle inhabited by headhunters, the headhunters' goal of killing John invokes a new preservation goal in John to preserve his life, and this is the goal with which their goal is competing. Alternatively, it might be that the headhunters only wish to stop John from crossing the jungle, in which case their goal competes with John's original goal.

In any case, to prevent creating a goal in another planner that will compete with a goal of one's own, a planner may pick some part of the chain of events illustrated in Fig. 9.1, and change the circumstances of his plan so that the opponent's goal is not created as hypothesized. The strategies for doing so involve executing one's intended actions in such a way that one's opponent does not perceive these actions as indicative of the planner's actual intentions. Thus applying *CHANGE-CIR-CUMSTANCE* to avoiding competition gives rise to an additional goal of preventing one's intentions from becoming known. I label this goal *CONCEAL-PURPOSE*.

9.3.1.1 ADJUNCT GOALS

CONCEAL-PURPOSE is one of a special class of goals called *adjunct goals*. An adjunct goal is a goal that a planner has only because he is pursuing a plan for some other goal. Adjunct goals are similar to "secondary tasks" in McDermott's terminology (McDermott, 1977). For example, *CONCEAL-PURPOSE* is an adjunct goal because one only has a purpose to conceal if there already is another goal present. Adjunct goals differ from "primary goals," or goals that descend directly from themes, in two important ways:

Scenario for Anticipated Goal Competition   **Figure 9.1**

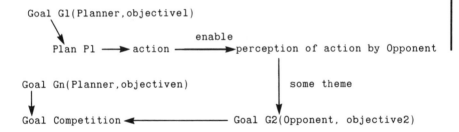

1. They come into being only when another goal is already present.

2. Plans for fulfilling adjunct goals are to a large degree a function of other plans and goals. Moreover, these plans generally work by specifying the mode in which some other action should be performed, rather than specifying an action of their own. Such plans are called adjunct plans.

For example, suppose a planner needs to sneak past some guards as he escapes from prison. He might execute this plan by wearing dark clothing and choosing the nighttime for his escape. However, this tactic is parasitic on a plan that gets the planner out of prison—the planner must still climb a wall, go through a door, and so on in order to get out, in addition to avoiding detection. In other words, he must perform some action that is normally construed as a plan for his original goal of changing his location. His adjunct plan merely prevents this action from having certain undesirable consequences.

The importance of distinguishing an adjunct goal from a primary goal lies in the applicable planning strategies. The primary planning distinction is that one would not entertain a scenario fulfilling an adjunct goal but jeopardizing the goal to which it is subservient. Such a scenario may be considered in the case of two primary goals in conflict; but abandoning a primarily goal to fulfill an adjunct goal is equivalent to abandoning a high-level goal to fulfill one of its subgoals, a thoroughly senseless enterprise.

9.3.1.2 *CONCEAL-PURPOSE* **Strategies**

CONCEAL-PURPOSE occurs as an adjunct goal. The strategies for accomplishing this goal are instances of those strategies used to prevent some hypothesized future from being actualized. As Fig. 9.1 suggests, the hypothesized future to be prevented contains the following general sequence of events:

1. Opponent perceives some event involving the planner.

2. Opponent infers motivation of planner based on this perception and other available information.

To disrupt this sequence from having its undesirable effect, one may prevent the perception of the planner altogether, disguise this perception so that the opponent draws an incorrect conclusion about the planner's motive, or supply the opponent with information that would make him conclude that the event he perceives arose from a goal he would not oppose.

Thus I hypothesize three subclasses of methods, which I call *PREVENT-PERCEPTION*, *ALTER-PERCEPTION*, and *GIVE-FALSE-MOTIVATION*. The *PREVENT-PERCEPTION* strategy involves executing one's plan so as not to be perceived at all. *ALTER-PERCEPTION* works by causing the action to be perceived, but as something other than what it is. *GIVE-FALSE-MOTIVATION* conceals one's purpose by explicitly supplying one's opponent with an incorrect (but plausible) explanation for one's actions.

Before we examine these strategies in more detail, it is important to point out that they do not exhaust the variety of anticipated goal competition situations. This is because not all such situations require one's goals to be detected by an opponent. For example, a fugitive may invoke a competitive goal in a law officer simply by being recognized. Thus strategies to prevent recognition are applicable as well. These are clustered into a category called **CONCEAL-IDENTITY**. While there is a significant amount of knowledge involved in this category, it is rather specific to themes that require knowledge of an identity to function. Likewise, other individual themes may each have their own requirements that allow specific forms of planning. However, the **CONCEAL-PURPOSE** cluster appears to be much more general, as it is applicable independent of the theme involved. Thus it merits special attention in the analysis.

9.3.1.3 *PREVENT-PERCEPTION*

In the **PREVENT-PERCEPTION** strategy, the planner performs his plan in such a mode as to make detection difficult. Exactly how this can be done depends primarily on the mode of perception that the planner anticipates will be involved in the detection of his action. If the planner anticipates being seen, he may use a quite different sort of concealment than he would if he expects to be heard or detected by radar. Nevertheless, some general kinds of methods apply throughout. Observe that for an object to be perceived by a particular sense, the following conditions must hold:

1. *The sense faculty must be operative.*
2. *The event to be perceived must fall within certain parameters.*

Within this subclass are several specific planning strategies: the planner can arrange for the sense faculty to the inoperative at the time the plan is executed, or the planner can execute his plan in such a manner that it is not detectable by that sense. This gives rise to two main methods: **NEUTRALIZE-SENSORY-CAPACITY** and **CIRCUMVENT-SENSORY-CAPACITY**.

NEUTRALIZE-SENSORY-CAPACITY is used in story (9.7)a where the planner chooses to execute his original plan at a time when the anticipated mode of detection is expected to function poorly. This is just the application of the general procedure of waiting for a desired condition to come about of its own accord. Alternatively, a more aggressive form of **NEUTRALIZE-SENSORY-CAPACITY** would be to take some action to render the sense ineffective. Thus a planner could shine a bright light into the eye of the observer, jam the opponent's radar, create a smoke screen, and so on. Clearly, particular knowledge of how the individual sense functions is needed at this point.

Much of this knowledge is compiled into canned plans. For example, creating a smoke screen is not something one is likely to invent, but rather this is a canned plan for   NEUTRALIZE-SENSORY-CAPACITY   as applied to visual perception. No doubt there are many such specific plans for each sense in addition to the more general strategy.

An alternative to this strategy is the plan ***CIRCUMVENT-SENSORY-CAPACITY***. Like ***NEUTRALIZE-SENSORY-CAPACITY***, this plan has a great deal of internal structure to it. Here a planner tries to circumvent a functioning sensory capacity by taking advantage of its limitations. For example, the visual sense requires a focusing in the direction of the object perceived; thus two strategies to circumvent visual detection are to wait for one's opponent to be looking the other way, or to encourage him to do so by creating a diversion or by giving him some other reason to attend his senses elsewhere. The latter is the method used in story (9-7)c. Again these are just passive and active versions of the same basic scheme. In addition, one could try to prevent the perceptual quality detectable by that sense from being generated. Thus if the primary mode of detection were auditory, one might wear gym shoes and walk softly. As was the case earlier, both sense-specific knowledge and circumvention plans are applicable at this point.

One particularly important consideration in the application of ***CIRCUMVENT-SENSORY-CAPACITY*** involves fitting actions into prearranged time slices. For example, if a planner waits for his opponent to look the other way in order to get somewhere undetected, the planner must get across before the opponent turns back. Thus the planner must not only wait for the appropriate moment to execute his plan, but he must execute it in such a way as to complete it in a specific period of time. This is part of the more general problem of executing a plan within a time constraint. The strategies available here are to either pick a plan that requires only the allowable amount of time or execute a potentially more lengthly plan in a hurried mode. Story (9-7)b is an example of this strategy.

Using the terminology introduced earlier, I define an adjunct goal called ***MEET-TIME-CONSTRAINT***. In effect, I consider all goals involving deadlines to be two goals, namely, "achieve state X" along with "finish plan for achieving state X by time T." Adjunct plans for this goal include scheduling the plan for the primary goal to begin early enough and executing that plan at a fast enough pace.

The advantage of thinking about such goals in this way is that it allows one to store plans for each goal separately and then deal with their interactions. For example, the goal of having a quarterly report in on time can be accomplished by choosing a plan for getting a quarterly report done, and then making sure that this plan is completed early enough. If a plan for getting a quarterly report done is to write it, and if a plan for getting something done in a short time period is to do it quickly, the resulting reasonable plan of writing the report quickly can be computed.

Similarly, if the plan to get by one's opponent is to cross while his head is turned, one needs to execute a plan for crossing with the adjunct goal of executing this plan before one's opponent turns back. If a plausible plan to cross is to do so under one's own power, the ***MEET-TIME-CONSTRAINT*** adjunct goal can give rise to the strategy of running across at the proper moment.

Of course, any number of these strategies can be executed simultaneously. Thus it is possible to run across in sneakers after creating a diversion and making a smoke screen. The only potential difficulties here are the unusual interactions between plans, which are to be handled in the manner I have been describing throughout. In particular, some of these strategies may have undesirable consequences of their own that need to be taken into account. For example, some plans to neutralize an opponent's senses will also inform him that someone is planning against him. This may have to be taken into consideration along with the possible benefits of that strategy.

9.3.1.4 *ALTER-PERCEPTION*

An alternative to ***PREVENT-PERCEPTION*** is to allow oneself to be detected as long as the nature of one's true action is concealed. This is the ***ALTER-PERCEPTION*** strategy. It is instantiated in story (9-7)d. As is the case for ***PREVENT-PERCEPTION*** strategies, these are adjunct plans that contain enough structure to combine successfully with basic-level plans to produce plans of action appropriate to a given situation.

Various disguise and camouflage techniques fit in here, and, as before, specific knowledge of the mode of perception is needed. Canned plans abound; for example, military-style camouflage is a canned plan to avoid detection in the course of a military operation by making one's forces look something like their surroundings.

9.3.1.5 *GIVE-FALSE-MOTIVATION*

The third technique for ***CONCEAL-PURPOSE*** is ***GIVE-FALSE-MOTIVATION***. This plan involves supplying one's opponent with a convenient explanation for one's actions that will not cause one's opponent to generate an undesirable goal. For example, John fooling the natives into thinking he was bringing them gifts in story (9-7)e is an instance of this plan.

Note that John's plan works here because it possesses several characteristics. It supplies a false motive that is consistent with his intended action; in this case, he intended to walk across the jungle, and his false motive also required him to do so. Second, the motive is something amenable to his opponent. Had he used a false motive that also generated a competitive goal, he would be of course no better off than before he chose to deceive. In fact, the motive he used in the example would actually encourage the natives to facilitate John's goal. Finally, John had to communicate his invention to the natives in some fashion.

Thus ***GIVE-FALSE-MOTIVATION*** can be broken down into two main subparts: generating the useful fiction, and conveying it to the anticipated antagonist.

9.3.1.5.1 *GENERATE-ALTERNATIVE-SCENARIO*

First, a scenario must be created. Since it is necessary that the scenario be believable and conducive to the planner's goals, the proposed scenario must meet the following constraints:

> *1. It must be consistent with the planner's intended actions.*
> *2. It must not invoke an undesirable goal in one's opponent.*

The mechanism for executing this plan is the same as that used to resolve goal conflicts. Recall that the ***REPLAN*** meta-plan for resolving works by first using ***MAKE-ATTRIBUTION*** to find the cause of the problem, and then doing an intelligent memory fetch to find a plan applicable to the goal in question but without the undesirable property extracted by ***MAKE-ATTRIBUTION***. If it fails to find one directly, a more costly generate-and-test strategy may be used.

To execute ***GENERATE-ALTERNATIVE-SCENARIO***, one first needs to know the cause of the problem. Thus one uses ***MAKE-ATTRIBUTION*** to find the problem with the proposed plan. Note that generally the problem is known, but ***MAKE-ATTRIBUTION*** is necessary to find a useful characterization. For example, suppose a planner is considering robbing a bank but needs to know the location of the safe deposit boxes. If he came in with his true motivation known, his plan is not likely to succeed. However, ***MAKE-ATTRIBUTION*** can be used to specify a precise problem, such as the bank learning that the planner is a robber when it stops and questions him as he tries to approach the safe deposit boxes. Thus the planner can now seek a scenario in which he is not identified in his actual role.

Having determined the plan characteristic to be avoided, the planner must now find a plan consistent with his intended actions but which does not possess this characteristic. This is analogous to the memory search in ***TRY-ALTERNATE-PLAN***, except that here one seeks a goal motivating an action. This is in fact the kind of explanatory mechanism needed for story understanding. That is, we can view the planner as thinking about the events he is about to precipitate as story actions requiring explanation. The only constraint is that the explanation he develops not include a plan that possesses the undesirable characteristic specified by ***MAKE-ATTRIBUTION***. In the case of the robber getting to see the safe deposit boxes, the planner needs to come up with an explanation for wanting to see the boxes that doesn't involve being identified as a robber. A possible explanation for going to see a safe deposit box is that one is a customer and wishes to use one, or that one is a bank inspector. In either case, the scenario does not lead to the undesirable consequence of being identified as a thief. Thus the planner can adopt either scenario.

Of course, the planner must still check that his proposed scenario is not undesirable in some other way. ***MAKE-ATTRIBUTION*** can only specify that the same problem inherent in the actual motive be avoided. Thus it is necessary to project the consequences of the proposed alibi to make sure it is no worse than the truth. For example, telling one's spouse one is late because he murdered his boss may avoid the unpleasant consequences of telling the truth, but is unlikely to be a good strategy because of its own consequences.

As is also the case in goal conflict resolution, if no entirely suitable plan can be found, the consequences of executing one of these plans is considered vis-à-vis the benefits. **SIMULATE-AND-SELECT** can therefore be used to choose the most appropriate alibi or to eliminate this option altogether if a satisfactory one cannot be found.

9.3.1.5.2 *PROJECT-SCENARIO*

Once the false motive is selected, the planner must make his opponent believe it. This is done by actually executing the proposed scenario. One simply plays the role specified for him in the scenario as closely as possible. For example, if the bank robber tries to pass himself off as a bank inspector, he dresses as a bank inspector, obtains false papers, and goes through the motions of doing some sort of inspection.

The only additional planning device needed here is the notion of simulating an appearance. That is, the planner must both appear and act as his role requires. For example, to play the role of the bank inspector, one may need official-looking documents. One may infer this as follows: In the false scenario, the planner projects himself having to show his credentials to a bank official. Since he plans to execute this scenario, his ordinary planning apparatus informs him that he will need to have credentials as this is instrumental to carrying out his plan. However, since the point of this action is to convince one's opponent of the false motive, it is sufficient to obtain some object that appears to his opponent to be the actual object required. As another example, the jungle traveler deceiving the natives by pretending to bring them presents could use empty boxes, or tell the natives that the presents will be coming down the river in a couple of days.

GENERATE-ALTERNATIVE-SCENARIO together with **PROJECT-SCENARIO** is a useful strategy for deception in general, and is not confined to conveying an incorrect motive for one's actions. For example, pretending that a toy gun is a real gun may enable one to establish a credible threat. Hence one does not disguise one's motives but instead one is able to carry out a plan without meeting all of its usual preconditions.

Many forms of deception seem to fit into this structure. In addition to the bluffing strategy just mentioned, making a false promise, such as offering to trade something that one doesn't own, also consists of producing a believable scenario and then giving the appearance of carrying it out, as does generating a consistent alibi.

Executing a **PROJECT-SCENARIO** plan may lead to some undesirable consequences, as is suggested by the following anecdote. Two men were in the locker room changing into their golfing clothes when one of them noticed the other putting on a girdle. Curious about this unusual piece of sporting equipment, he asked his friend how long he had been wearing a girdle when he played golf. "Ever since my wife found it in the glove compartment of my car" was the response.

9.3.1.6 MIXED STRATEGIES

In the preceding discussion of tactics to protect against an opponent knowing one's goal, it was generally assumed that the strategies are applied in isolation. However, they may often be used in conjunction with one another. For example, a planner that supplies a false motive still has to carry out the steps of his original plan, and some of these steps may not be masked by that motivation and may need to be concealed further. Thus the thief entering the bank disguised as an inspector may wait until he is alone in order to take photographs, as this would not be explanable via his adopted role.

In general, the most complicated interactions occur between ***CONCEAL-PURPOSE*** and the other strategies. This is because adopting a particular ***CONCEAL-PURPOSE*** strategy depends on the degree with which the proposed false motive allows the actions unaccounted for to be undetected. For example, a bank inspector may have the prerogative of being left alone in the vault, while an ordinary customer may not. This would therefore be a better alibi if concealing an action still remained to be done. In principle, the overall model of projecting one's current plans into the future allows for these strategies to mix. Thus simulating the scenario of impersonating a customer may leave one with a problem of how to take photos undetected. Either this flaw in the proposed plan can be dealt with and the simulation continued or the alternative scenario of impersonating the inspector can be considered.

In sum, although on the surface Independent Plan Alteration does not explicitly refer to the notion of competition, the meta-plans for goal conflict may have to make use of knowledge about competition to suggest an appropriate change in the circumstances or to suggest a canned plan for the situation at hand.

9.3.2 Induced Plan Alteration

In the previous section, we examined methods of avoiding competition by altering one's own plans. An alternative possibility is to get one's competitors to alter their plans so as not to collide with one's own. For example, consider the following stories.

(9- 8)   John wanted to watch the football game on TV but Mary wanted to watch the ballet.
(a) John asked Mary if she would watch the ballet at her mother's.
(b) John told Mary he would take her out to the ballet if she didn't watch the ballet on TV.
(c) John said he would be willing to watch half the game and Mary could watch half the ballet.
(d) John told Mary that her mother got sick and was taken to the hospital.

Each of these scenarios involves a method of persuading someone to do what one wants. In (9-8)a, the planner tries asking; in (9-8)b and (9-8)c, bargaining; and in (9-8)d, a method of tricking one's opponent into making a decision beneficial to one's interest.

The techniques for induced plan alteration are essentially those of the *persuade package* discussed by Schank and Abelson (1977). These are the plans for convincing someone to do something. A planner wishing an opponent to alter his plans for one's convenience may use one or more of these methods to persuade him to do so. This strategy has two parts:

1. Generating a scenario one would want one's opponent to adopt.
2. Persuading one's opponent to adopt it.

The problem of scenario generation is essentially that dealt with in the previous section. Here one needs to come up with a scenario for one's opponent that still fulfills his goals but at the same time avoids competition with one's own. The method just described applies as well.

There are several interesting complications here, however. One is that independent plan alteration and induced plan alteration often interact in the form of bargaining. That is, the bargain plan works by offering one's opponent something of value to him in order to persuade him to some end. Doing so in effect usually entails that the planner abandon some less important goal of his own. For example, offering someone money to do something means abandoning a possession.

Partially abandoning competing goal is something that one can offer to an opponent. For example, if Russia and the U.S. both want control of Europe, they might agree to divide it between themselves. In terms of the analysis here, this situation consists of each party partially abandoning their original goal (i.e., world domination) in order to partially achieve this goal while avoiding competition.

This combined strategy is called *mutual induced abandonment.* It is equivalent to the notion of bargaining if one interprets that to include the details of negotiation and compromise. In effect, mutual induced abandonment may be considered a fine grain analysis of why this particular method of persuasion works and how one actually employs it. The method is simply generating a scenario that one's competitor might accept, and which is of optimum value to the planner, iterating this process and communicating this scenario to one's opponent, until a proposal is accepted. All the details of compromising are just this strategy, using goal abandonment as one of the currencies of exchange.

A second complication occurs when one uses the persuade package to deceive someone, as in story (9-8)d. Again, this is a standard plan for cheating someone, but our analysis explains how to actually use it and why. The method is the same as that used to deceive someone so as to avoid generating a competitive goal. Namely, one uses ***GENERATE-ALTERNATIVE-SCENARIO*** together with ***PROJECT-SCENARIO*** to cause one's opponent to take the desired action.

9.3.2.1 COMPARISON WITH CARBONELL'S DIVERSIONARY
COUNTER-PLANNING

In his analysis of interactions of goals across individuals, Carbonell considers some of these strategies under the heading of "diversionary counter-planning" (Carbonell, 1979). He describes a set of specific methods of focusing one's opponent's attention elsewhere. In the analysis presented here, I prefer not to create a separate category for such plans. Instead, the same methods are derived in the organization from more general considerations.

Basically Carbonell's diversion strategies work by causing the opponent to believe that he has another goal, which is in conflict with the first and which may be more important. However, causing someone to have a more significant goal is a general way of persuading, and is applicable in situations not involving goal competition per se. For example, telling a lifeguard that someone is drowning is a way of getting the lifeguard to rescue that person, although it is unlikely that the situation should be analyzed in terms of goal competition.

Other forms of persuasion also work this way, for example, making an explicit threat against someone. In my analysis, Carbonell's diversionary tactics are an application of the general notion of creating an alternative scenario and getting one's opponent to adopt it. Similarly, the trick options described by Carbonell fall out of the general notion of using deception to persuade someone. The primary advantage of my approach is that it is generative, that is, all knowledge about persuasion is immediately applicable to induced goal abandonment, without having to precompile this knowledge into rules specific to goal competition.

This difference between Carbonell's formulation of this particular piece of knowledge and the formulation I prefer is characteristic of an important difference in our approaches. I will illustrate this difference again in several other areas in which the knowledge we characterize is similar.

As the various methods of persuasion have been discussed elsewhere (for example, in Schank and Abelson, 1977), I shall not labor them here.

9.4 COMPETITIVE PLAN EXECUTION

The second major class of strategies involved in goal competition applies to those situations in which the planners engage in explicit, competitive actions. Induced plan alteration is related to this category, but in that class of situations the focus is on avoiding confrontation. Here the focus is on winning a confrontation.

The strategies for competitive plan execution are generally referred to as *anti-plans*. This term was first used by James Meehan in an unpublished manuscript. I use it here in a manner similar to Carbonell's use of the term "counter-planning" (Carbonell, 1979). One difference in the terminology is that counter-planning refers to the general set of strategies involved in goal competition, including the various strategies for goal abandonment detailed earlier. I use anti-planning to refer only to those strategies involved in executing a plan in a competitive situation. I believe that these differences in nomenclature are primarily reflective of differences in organization rather than of fundamental incompatibility. In any case, much of the analysis presented by Carbonell is of relevance here.

To examine the structure of anti-plans, consider the following stories.

(9- 9) *John was hoping he would be promoted to the regional manager position that just opened up. Then John learned that Bill was also a contender for the job.*
(a) John tried to perform his own job better than Bill performed his.
(b) John decided to try to curry favor with the boss.
(c) John spread some nasty rumors about Bill around the company.
(d) John sneaked into Bill's office one night and stole some papers Bill needed to get his report in on time.

These situations consist of two groups. In (9-9)a and (9-9)b, the planner tries to fulfill his own goal simply by pursuing the plans he might use anyway. Thus John might have tried to do his job well even if there were no competitors; in the competitive situation he tries to do this better than his rival. In addition, although one might not have bothered to develop a rapport with one's boss if the competition had not merited such measures, this is still a plan one might employ if no competition were present. In (9-9)c and (9-9)d, on the other hand, John uses the strategy of undermining his opponent. Rather than make himself look good, John tries to make his rival look bad. Note that these strategies do not ensure John his goal directly, but only do so by diminishing the effectiveness of his rival.

These two groups are instances of the two major classes of anti-planning strategies:

   1. OUT-DO—The planner attempts to perform an action so as to do better than his opponents. Situations (9-9)a and (9-9)b are instances of this strategy.
   2. UN-DO—The planner executes a plan so as to make his opponents' plans more difficult to be successfully executed. Situations (9-9)c and (9-9)d embody this kind of planning.

9.4.1 *OUT-DO*

OUT-DO is employed by executing plans for one's own goal so as to be more effective than one's opponent. As such, *OUT-DO* is actually an instance of a more general meta-planning strategy describing how to select a plan for a goal in the first place. To demonstrate this point, we must first consider the structure of plans and the architecture of the basic planning mechanism in more detail.

According to the model, when faced with a goal, the planner proposes a plan for this goal, and then evaluates this plan through the projection process. The projection process may involve filling in of some details of the plan, such as the values of unspecified parameters. For example, suppose a planner wishes to move a desk across the room, and that the plan it first proposes for this task is to push the desk. For this plan to work, the planner must push the desk with sufficient force. That is, the plan of moving something by pushing it must be stored as something like "push the object with enough force to make it move." Thus the "push plan" has a parameter corresponding to the level of force applied, and a constraint that this parameter be set above a certain threshold.

This constraint translates into the prerequisite of being able to apply sufficient force. Prerequisites are routinely examined during the projection phase to understand what it would be like to execute the plan. Generally, this is how the need to fulfill a subgoal is determined. For example, in the case of pushing an object, the planner must determine whether he has sufficient strength. This may be done by a number of means, for example, by estimating the force required and the force which the planner can generate, by finding a similar attempt in memory and examining the result, or by finding some chain of reasoning about the force needed and available. An example of the last category might be "I once pushed a larger desk, so I should be able to push this smaller one."

If this process finds that the prerequisite can be met, a by-product of the computation is a statement about the value of the parameter. This may be used to inform the planner about the approximate level of effort he should supply during execution. If projection finds that the prerequisite cannot be met, the plan fails in the simulation and various meta-plans go into effect to try to remedy the problem. For example, **CHANGE-CIRCUMSTANCE** might propose putting the object on rollers and then proceeding with the original plan.

In sum, some of the preconditions of a plan are a function of the context in which that plan is to be used. The **OUT-DO** strategy is essentially a technique for evaluating a precondition and establishing the value of a parameter when one of the considerations is the presence of a competitor. For example, in the case of being promoted, the stored plan might be "do your job well enough." In a noncompetitive situation, "well enough" may be determined to be "well enough to please the boss." However, in the presence of competition, the **OUT-DO** strategy specifies that "well enough" means "better than my competitor." Again, depending on what is known in the situation, this might be further reduced to a specific value or left in this intentional form.

As in the case of noncompetitive parameter-fixing, the planner might find that he cannot achieve a high enough value of the parameter in the proposed plan to get it to work. In this case, the same strategy that is used in noncompetitive situations may be applied. Namely, the planner might try a new plan or change the circumstances surrounding his old one. Thus in the example of the planner trying to get a promotion, suppose the planner conjectures that he could not out-perform his opponent. Then he might decide to change his plan to curry favor with the boss, or to do this along with trying to out-work his opponent, or to making an alliance with a fellow worker to aid him in his performance. The point of all these considerations is that the **OUT-DO** tactic is essentially just the application of more basic planning principles applied to the case of determining the value of a parameter in the presence of competition.

To further illustrate how this works, consider the following stories.

(9-10)   John and Bill were rivals for Mary's heart. John tried to convince Mary that he would make a better husband for her than Bill would.

(9-11)   John and Bill both wanted to win the high hurdles. They each ran as fast as they could.

(9-12)   John was afraid that Bill would out-work John and get the promotion John wanted. John decided it would be a good idea to marry the boss's daughter.

Story (9-10) is a straightforward instance of fixing a parameter in the context of competition. A plan for getting someone to marry you may be to convince that person that you will make a good spouse. How good a spouse you will be is a parameter to be fixed. In the presence of a competitor, this value is fixed at "better than one's rival." Then this instance of the plan is executed.

In some instances, the appropriate value of a parameter will remain unknown until execution. In these instances, some heuristic is needed to guess at the best value. This is apparently the case in story (9-11). Here each planner probably estimates that he will need a great deal of effort to fulfill his goal, and thus uses all the power available to him in the execution of his plan.

In story (9-12), the planner believes that the plan he selected will not work unaided. Thus the general planning mechanism is brought into play, and proposes supplementing the current plan with additional measures to enhance the possibility of success.

9.4.1.1   TIME CONSTRAINTS AND *OUT-DO*

In addition to fixing parameters such as effort, **OUT-DO** may also have important effects on the time parameters of a plan. As was discussed in a previous chapter on goal conflict, each goal has a time period during which a plan for that goal must be executed in order to have a chance of success. In general, this interval of initiation may be a function of the context in which the plan is executed. If there is another planner with a competing goal, his fulfillment of that goal will undo a precondition for one's own plan. Thus the time period within which one can expect to successfully execute a plan for one's own goal is constrained to end before the competitor completes execution of his plan, i.e., one must fulfill one's goal before one's competitor does.

The application of the **OUT-DO** strategy therefore produces a time constraint on one's plan, the constraint being that the plan be completed before one's opponent's. Recall that time constraints are handled by the attachment of adjunct goals.

Thus if I determine that I have to get to New York before John does, I will represent this as the goal of getting to New York with the adjunct goal of getting there before John. Depending on my assessment of the time period this allows, I might end up executing a particular plan, like flying, or executing another plan in a hurried mode, such as driving fast. (Incidentally, the situations involving force rather than time are not handled with adjunct plans because they are not as easily decomposable as those involving time constraints. That is, a plan for getting somewhere fast may be decomposed into a plan for getting somewhere plus the constraint that the plan meet a deadline; a plan for moving an object *cannot* be decomposed into a plan for pushing plus some constraint because pushing without regard to force is not in and of itself a plan for anything.)

Contrast this approach with that offered by Carbonell (1979). He tends to include such considerations as explicit rules. For example, he states the rule that "IF X can achieve G (X) before Y can achieve G (Y), THEN X should plan to pursue G (X) at the earliest possible opportunity." This is essentially the knowledge just described, the only difference being that in my formulation, the knowledge is derivable from more general considerations, namely, from the *OUT-DO* strategy and knowledge of ordinary plan application, and no explicit rule is needed.

Of course, this is not to say that such a rule would not be useful—redundant rules may constitute a good time-space tradeoff. Rather, the advantage of formulation given here is that it is more general, i.e., that it will apply to parameters other than time without having to make up new explicit rules. In addition, the specific rules do not explain why the planner should do what they recommend, and therefore they are difficult to use for more general reasoning. For example, consider Carbonell's rule just given. Suppose it is the case that the planner knows of two plans for a goal, one which is very costly but can be executed right away, and another that is quite inexpensive but which cannot be executed until sometime later. However, assume that both can be executed at some time before one's opponent can take any relevant action. The rule will prefer the expensive plan, but for no good reason. However, the more general strategy I suggest will not show a preference for this plan, and the cheaper plan will be selected *ceteris paribus*.

Part of the problem is that Carbonell's rule is slightly flawed. It should read something like "IF X can achieve G (X) before Y can achieve G (Y), THEN X should plan to pursue G (X) before Y can achieve G (Y)." That is, there is no hurry to start right away, only to get done first. However, the core of the problem still remains. For example, the rule could not be used to inform the planner that he should execute his plan quickly—this is implied by the motivation for the rule, but is not inferable from the rule per se.

Mostly, my argument is for the necessity of the general knowledge presented here, rather than against specific rules such as those presented by Carbonell. As before, I assume that the planner uses such specific rules and retreats to more general principles as the situation warrants. I focus on the more general forms because they are essential for certain situations and are sufficient for the function subsumed by more specific rules in other analyses.

9.4.2 *UNDO*

In the previous section, I argued that the presence of competition may influence the manner in which one executes a plan for a goal, but that this influence may be computed and understood by the mechanism presupposed for noncompetitive plan execution. That is, the *OUT-DO* strategy is an instance of the more general notion of mustering enough resources together to execute a plan successfully.

An additional strategy for fulfilling a goal in the presence of competition is to undermine the efforts of one's opponent. These strategies are much more specific to goal competition. Consider the following stories.

(9-13) *Both Russia and the US were trying to win over Egypt to their camp.*
(a) The US tried to convince the Egyptians that the Russians couldn't be trusted.
(b) The Russians planted false documents showing that the US had conspired to overthrow the Egyptian regime.

Examples (9-13)a and (9-13)b represent measures taken to hinder one's opponent's plan. One way for a country to win over another is to gain that nation's confidence. The US, anticipating this attempt in (9-13)a, takes a measure to undermine such trust. Similarly, the Russians execute a plan in (9-13)b to make it more difficult for the US to cozy up to the Egyptians.

I call such plans *UN-DO* strategies. Unlike *OUT-DO* methods, *UN-DO* strategies generally do not result in achieving one's goal; rather, they make it possible to achieve a goal by eliminating the competition. Thus, in examples (9-13)a and (9-13)b, either or both countries might succeed in their *UN-DO* strategy but still fail in their goal. The Russians might convince the Egyptians that the Americans were out to get them, for example, but still fail to convince the Egyptians that they themselves are good allies.

UN-DO works by setting up an adjunct goal of preventing one's opponent from achieving his goal state. The goal is an adjunct to the more primary goal that generated the competition. Thus in story (9-13), both the US and Russia have the adjunct goal of preventing the other from becoming allies with Egypt; this goal is an adjunct to each country's primary goal of getting Egypt to join its camp.

Of course, it may be the case that the plan for preventing one's opponent from achieving his goal is equivalent to the plan for fulfilling one's own. If an opponent causes you to have a preservation goal, blocking one's opponent is equivalent to fulfilling your preservation goal. An instance of this would be fending off a threat on one's life, in which the opponent's goal of killing you and your goal of surviving are simultaneously blocked and fulfilled, respectively. But this is only the case when the conflicting goals logically exclude one another. Much goal competition does not conform to this paradigm. Instead, each competitor's success entails the other's failure, but each competitor's failure does not usually entail the other's success. In any case this distinction will not present any special difficulty for the following analysis.

The plans for **UN-DO**ing the opposition are essentially plans for fulfilling preservation goals, where the cause of the goal is the intention of another planner. As such, it is convenient to divide these strategies into those for fulfilling preservation goals in general and those specific to preservation goals caused by another planner. For example, consider the following stories.

(9-14)   *Bill tried to kill John by pushing a boulder down on him. John jumped out of the way.*

(9-15)   *John wanted to prevent Bill from pushing the desk across the room. He ran around to the other side and pushed the other way.*

(9-16)   *John wanted to prevent Bill from marrying Mary. He started spreading nasty rumors about Bill around town.*

In stories (9-15) and (9-16), John tries to block Bill's plan, but John's action can be interpreted without special knowledge of competition. In both examples, the plan used would have been the same had the cause of the preservation goal been an inanimate force. However, in story (9-16), the action taken by John only makes sense if we consider that the situation to be prevented involves the plan of another agent. It is these sorts of situations that merit special attention within the **UN-DO** category.

The primary plan for preventing the successful completion of another's plan is called **UNDO-PRECONDITION**. This plan works by inferring the competitor's plan, and then removing a precondition necessary for its successful execution. For example, in story (9-16), John tries to foil Bill's plan to marry Mary by violating a prerequisite for this plan, namely, that a person think highly of a prospective spouse. (Actually, the complete analysis of the structure of John's plan, spreading a rumor, is somewhat more complicated, but within the realm of our current machinery. For example, if John told Mary bad things about Bill directly, she might suspect John's motives. Thus it is a good idea for John to keep his motives from Mary. John's action is therefore interpreted as a realization of an **UNDO-PRECONDITION** plan for lowering Mary's esteem for John, coupled with an adjunct **CONCEAL-PURPOSE** goal.)

One particular flavor of **UNDO-PRECONDITION** has to do with the *implicit preconditions* of a plan. These are the preconditions that are usually never considered because they are almost always true when they are needed. For example, being awake is a precondition for eating, but it is generally unnecessary to worry about it. Structurally, however, these preconditions bear exactly the same relationship to a plan as more commonly pursued preconditions.

In fact, it is just because such preconditions are so general that they play an important role in anti-planning. For example, **UNDO-PRECONDITION** can be applied to virtually any competitive situation by eliminating the other planner as an active agent. That is, being a functioning animate agent is a precondition of every plan; thus undoing this precondition will work in any competitive situation. In any of the situations presented so far in this chapter, a plan that eliminates the agency planning to execute the offending plan is a workable instance of **UNDO-PRECONDITION**. Thus John can always kill Bill to prevent him from marrying Mary, or to prevent him from winning a race, and so on.

An agent can be incapacitated in a variety of ways, some of which will only be appropriate to specific plans. However, all such situations are encompassed by **UNDO-PRECONDITION** once we allow states like being alive or being awake as preconditions. The only problem in doing so is that we take care to separate these preconditions from the more usual ones. This is important because we do not want the planner to check to see that it is awake each time it simulates every proposed plan. One solution to this problem is to store these general preconditions at the proper place along an event hierarchy, and only check the preconditions specific to the particular plan in question. That is, a precondition like "being awake" is stored along with the category "action," to which all actions eventually are connect with ISA-type links. In ordinary planning, we only check those preconditions that are not inherited because these are the ones most likely to need attention, but in anti-planning we focus on the inherited preconditions because these are ones most likely to be applicable.

9.4.2.1 ANTI-ANTI-PLANNING, AND SO ON

One version of anti-planning not treated explicitly so far is countering someone's countermove, and so on. For example consider the following stories.

(9-17) *John and Bill were both bucking for the same promotion.*
(a) John expected that Bill would bad-mouth him to his boss, so he told his boss not to believe anything Bill said.
(b) Bill was afraid that John would tell the boss that he was a liar, and then his plan of bad-mouthing John wouldn't work. Bill made sure he got to the boss before John did.

In (9-17)a, John's action is an anti-plan against Bill's anti-plan of libeling John. Example (9-17)b goes one step further, with Bill anticipating John's anti-plan against his anti-plan, and anti-planning against this effort by trying to establish his credibility first.

Although these situations are ostensibly more complex than those examined earlier, they can be handled by precisely the same machinery. That is, they can all be accounted for in terms of a planner applying some anti-planning measure against another planner's competitive goal—the only difference is that here the competitive goal may have been generated in response to a goal of the first planner. In fact, most of these situations are simply instances of applying **UNDO-PRECONDITION** to a plan for another agent's **UNDO-PRECONDITION** plan. For example, John's getting to his boss before Bill is an attempt to undo a precondition for Bill's plan of bad-mouthing John, which itself is a plan to undo a precondition for John's plan to get promoted.

What appears to become complicated in this sort of planning is not the structure of the plans themselves, which has been accounted for, but remembering the details of all these relationships. For example, given knowledge of a domain like chess, the basic planning and anti-planning strategies I have described are in principle capable of accounting for the moves of the game. However, the planner or understander I have described so far would not necessarily play a particularly good game of chess because no attention has been paid to remembering or searching through the myriad relationships and hypothetical relationships that may arise in planning an appropriate move.

9.4.3 An Example

To illustrate how all these strategies may apply to a situation, I give an extended example and very briefly refer to the planning structures mentioned earlier to explain how the model would account for each aspect of the situation. Details are left to the reader.

(9-18)   *Ali wanted to become world heavyweight champion.*
          (a) Ali trained very hard for the title fight.
          (b) Ali tried to hit his opponent repeatedly with his jab.
          (c) Before the fight, Ali said some things to try to psych out his opponent.
          (d) Whenver his opponent tried to come after him, Ali covered up on the ropes.
          (e) Ali's opponent claimed that someone put a drug in his water.
          (f) Ali's manager loosened the ropes around the ring so that Ali would be able to duck better.
          (g) Some big gamblers tried to prevent Ali from reaching the ring on the day of the big fight.

    Analysis:

    *1. (a) This is explained as fulfilling a precondition of the **OUT-DO** strategy applied to the plan for fighting.*
    2. (b) This action is the execution of that portion of the plan directly related to achieving one's goal, as opposed to preventing one's opponent from doing the same.
    *3. (c) **UNDO-PRECONDITION**, where the precondition involves mental attitude.*
    *4. (d) **UNDO-PRECONDITION**, here used to fend off opponent rather than to make it easier to succeed in one's high-level goal.*
    *5. (e) **UNDO-PRECONDITION** again.*
    *6. (f) This time, fulfilling a precondition for an **UNDO-PRECONDITION**.*
    *7. (g) **UNDO-PRECONDITION**, aimed here at an implicit precondition.*

9.5 SPONTANEOUS COMPLETION REMOVAL

As was the case for goal conflict, sometimes a problem may disappear of its own accord. Consider the following stories.

(9-19)   *John wanted to watch the football game, but Mary wanted to watch the ballet. Mary put on channel 3. She found out that the ballet was postponed until later that day.*

(9-20)   *John and Bill were stranded in the desert with only enough water for one of them to make it to the nearest town. Then they stumbled upon an oasis.*

In each case, a goal competition situation exists, but goes away for some reason other than as the result of an intention of one of the actors. In story (9-19), the problem disappears because one planner's plan cannot be executed, and in story (9-20), because the limited resource was spontaneously increased.

In terms of planning and understanding, the moral here is identical to that for spontaneous conflict resolution. That is, for that purpose, as well as for others, I demonstrated the need for a mechanism to track changes in the possibility of achieving a goal. By the same token, a planner needs to detect changes to the status of a competitive situation because, if a competitive goal goes away, a better course of action than the one currently slated may be available. For example, if a fairly costly action were planned to bring about a goal state because of the presence of a competitor, the **DON'T WASTE RESOURCES** meta-theme will cause this plan to be reconsidered in the event of spontaneous competition removal, as a cheaper plan may now be applicable.

9.6 SUMMARY

While goal competition is not quite so basic to the notion of planning as is goal conflict, it occupies a center stage if only because of the amount and importance of the knowledge it involves. I divided this knowledge into methods for eliminating competition and methods for winning competition. The first set of methods is largely an application of strategies we had encountered for goal conflict, although particular attention was given to methods for avoiding generating competitive goals. In particular, we examined strategies for concealing one's purpose. I introduced the notion of an adjunct goal, or a goal that exists only because of the existence of another goal.

The methods for winning a competition are divided into those directly aimed at fulfilling one's own goal and those aimed at hindering an opponent. The former work by specifying a set of constraints for a plan, such as that it must be executed with a certain amount of force or within a certain period of time. The latter include some general methods of dealing with preservation goals, and in addition, the anti-plan of undoing the preconditions of an opponent's plan.

10

Positive Goal Relationships

10.1 INTRODUCTION

Positive goal relationships are those goal interactions that yield some potential benefit to a planner. As is the case for negative goal relationships, positive goal relationships are divided into internal and external categories. *Goal overlap* is the term applied to positive goal relationships within an individual, and *goal concord* is applied to positive goal relationships across several planners.

In the case of an internal positive goal relationship, or goal overlap, a planner is able to carry out an action that is in the service of a number of goals at once. This might involve executing a single plan that simultaneously fulfills several goals, achieving a goal that serves more than one higher purpose, or employing a plan that is worthwhile only when a sufficient number of similar goals is involved. Each of these possibilities constitutes a distinguishable subcategory of goal overlap.

External positive goal relationships, or goal concord, describe interactions in which two or more planners have similar goals. Such interactions give rise to a number of planning strategies. For example, planners with concordant goals may work together, dividing up subtasks; they may pool resources and achieve goals that neither could attain independently; and they may expect to come to each other's aid in adverse situations when such actions would otherwise be unwarranted.

10.2 GOAL OVERLAP

Consider the following stories:

(10- 1) *John needed some wood finisher. While he was at the hardware store, he picked up some sandpaper.*

(10- 2) *John thought he could use some exercise. He also felt like he needed some fresh air, so he decided to go jogging in the park.*

(10- 3) *John moved out to the suburbs. He would be commuting to his job in the city everyday, so he decided to buy a car.*

Each of these stories describes a situation in which the simultaneous pursuit of the planner's goals is more advantageous than their independent pursuit. For example, in (10-1), considering the goals together allows the planner to make one trip to the store rather than two; in (10-2), it allows the planner to select a single plan that fulfills both goals; in (10-3), an indefinite number of recurring goals are addressed by a single step.

In all such goal overlap situations, the operative meta-theme is **DON'T WASTE RESOURCES**. That is, a goal overlap situation provides an opportunity to achieve goals more economically than they could be achieved otherwise. This principle is needed in order for the planner to prefer the selection of efficient plans over inefficient plans that otherwise achieve the planner's explicit goals. This principle would appear to be the underlying justification for a number of processes incorporated in other planning systems. For example, several of Sacerdoti's critics (Sacerdoti, 1977), including "use existing objects," "eliminate redundant preconditions," and "optimize disjuncts" are motivated by **DON'T WASTE RESOURCES** and correspond to particular kinds of goal overlap situations. Some of Sacerdoti's domain-dependent critics are also subsumed by the general treatment offered here.

For a general treatment of the strategies applicable to such situations, two kinds of goal overlap are distinguished:

1. Mutual Inclusion—The goals overlap by virtue of inherent relationships between the states constituting their realization.
2. Plan Overlap—The goals themselves have no inherent overlap, but some plan is applicable to more than one goal at once.

10.2.1 Mutual Inclusion

Mutual inclusion means that a planner has the same goal for more than one reason. Actually, the goals need not be literally identical, but may be in one of a number of relationships. Consider the following stories:

(10- 4) *John thought killing animals was morally wrong. He also thought that eating vegetables made one healthy.*
(10- 5) *John had to stay home because he expected a visitor. He also had to stay in his study because he was trying to write a paper.*

These examples contain two different kinds of similarity between goals: identity and entailment. In story (10-4), John has the goal of eating vegetables for two independent reasons. Thus the identical goal arises twice independently, producing a goal overlap situation. Alternatively one goal may be a specific instance of a more general goal. Story (10-5) is an instance of this case, as being in one's study is a special case of being in one's home via logical entailment.

To determine if two goals are identical, they merely need to be matched against one another. However, determining if one goal state implies the other requires some specific knowledge. For example, the fact that "A is inside B implies that A is inside C if B is part of C'' is needed to determine the relatedness of the goals in story (10-5). Of course, logical entailments can be arbitrarily complex. However, the everyday situations dealt with here seem to require only the straightforward application of heuristics such as the one just mentioned. A complete set of such heuristics remains a desirable goal.

Each type of relatedness has different consequences for a planner or understander:

    1. Identity—If the goals are in fact identical, simply follow a plan for the goal.

    2. Entailment—If one goal is implied by the other, pursue the implying goal. That is, if John needs to stay home and stay in his study, he should pursue the goal of staying in study.

In terms of meta-planning, the meta-goal triggered by **DON'T WASTE RE-SOURCES** in one of these situations is called *AVOID-REDUNDANT-GOALS*. It can be fulfilled by the meta-plan *USE-IDENTICAL-TASK-NETWORK*. This plan constrains the task networks that contain the two goals to intersect at a common goal. That is, the goal will appear only once, but will be referred to by all the task networks in which it plays a role.

10.2.2 Goal Subsumption

In mutual inclusion, multiple versions of essentially the same goal appear simultaneously. The applicable strategy is simply to treat all these as a single goal and to plan for it only once. However, multiple versions of the same goal may also occur serially in time. These cannot be treated collectively as a single element because they do not co-occur. Nevertheless a planner can take advantage of the recurrence of a goal to form a more efficient plan. For example, consider the following stories.

(10- 6)   *John got a job 50 miles from where he lived. He decided to buy a car.*
(10- 7)   *John got tired of going to a single's bar every night. He decided to get married.*

The plans in each of these cases are specific to situations involving recurring goals. For example, it would be unusual if someone decided to get married just because he didn't feel like going to a single's bar one evening. However, this plan is appropriate for the situation described in (10-7) because it provides a solution to a problem on a continuing basis.

Making it easier to fulfill a recurring goal is called *goal subsumption*. Goal subsumption involves the following components:

    1. A goal that arises repeatedly.
    2. A plan for this recurring goal.
    3. A state that fulfills a precondition for this plan and which endures over a time span that encompasses goal recurrences.

Thus in story (10-6), the recurring goal is one of transportation to work; the chosen plan is to drive a car; a precondition for this plan is to have control over a vehicle, and the state that fulfills this precondition is ownership of that vehicle. I call such a state of *goal subsumption state* and say that it subsumes the goal in question. Of course, since a plan can have more than one precondition, the same goal can be subsumed by more than one state.

Goal subsumption is different from mutual inclusion because the former entails an additional step that will be compensated for by its continued value. In contrast, in mutual inclusion situations, no additional planning steps are justified; instead, we merely recognize that duplicate goals should only be planned for once. That is, goal subsumption is a type of investment worth making because repetition is anticipated.

In terms of meta-planning elements, the meta-theme **DON'T WASTE RE-SOURCES** is again at work. The resources in danger of being wasted are those that would be involved in executing a plan repeatedly in order to fulfill a recurring goal. This meta-theme gives rise to the meta-goal ***SUBSUME-RECURRING-GOAL*** in situations in which the recurrence of a goal is anticipated. The meta-plan for this meta-goal is ***ESTABLISH-SUBSUMPTION-STATE***, that is, to set up a goal aimed at achieving a state that fulfills a precondition for a plan for the recurring goal and that endures over a period of time.

The value of a subsumption state is equivalent to the value of the precondition it fulfills, times the expected number of times it can be expected to fulfill it. This value must be balanced against the cost of establishing the subsumption state. However, for an important precondition of a frequently recurring goal, this value is essentially unlimited. It is therefore generally worthwhile to subsume a goal, *ceteris paribus.*

In particular, a subsumption state is most attractive when the current method of repeatedly fulfilling a precondition is expensive or undesirable. Thus the high cost or unpleasantness of a current plan is likely to precipitate the search for a plan that is less unpleasant, that is, to invoke the **DON'T WASTE RESOURCES** meta-theme to produce the goal of establishing a subsumption state. For example, consider the following story.

(10- 8)   John thought that commuting to work was a waste of energy. He decided to move into the city.

The negativity associated with the current plan for a recurring goal expressed in the first sentence activates the **DON'T WASTE RESOURCES** meta-theme and produces an attempt to find a subsumption state, which is realized in the second sentence of the example.

Sometimes an undesirable plan might already involve a subsumption state. For example, John might be using a car to commute in story (10-8). In this case, the new subsumption state replaces the old. This may in fact remove the justification for the old state entirely (e.g., John may now get rid of his car). This is part of a more general planning problem, in which the planner (or understander) must recognize that a state achieved in the service of a goal need no longer be maintained once the original goal is removed.

The value of a subsumption state is also important in reasoning about goal conflict. The existence of a subsumption state may conflict with some other goal, in which case, the value of that state as a subsumption state must be taken into account. For example, consider the following example.

(10- 9)   John loved his wife Mary, but their sex life was terrible.

Here the state of marriage subsumes a number of goals, but not all equally well. Thus there is a conflict between sustaining the marriage for its positive value as a subsumption state and violating it to fulfill other needs that are inadequately served. In resolving this conflict, the standard goal conflict resolution strategies can be used, with the value of the goal of sustaining the marriage encompassing the value inherited via its role as a subsumption state.

10.2.2.1 GOAL SUBSUMPTION SITUATIONS

As goal subsumption is a way of making it easier to fulfill a recurring goal, one situation in which it appears involves the establishment of a new goal. For example, consider the following story.

(10-10)   John enjoyed going to the Raider's games. He decided to buy a season's ticket.

A planner in this situation might behave this way if it reasoned as follows. Going to the Raider's games is an anticipated recurring goal, each occurrence of which involves having a ticket. Because having a season's ticket is a way of subsuming this goal, it may be an effective way to obtain the required tickets. Similarly an understander would interpret John's action as a plan to subsume a goal because buying a season's ticket is generally done as a means to subsume individual goals of attending football games. An explanation for having these individual goals is provided by the first sentence.

Another important situation in which goal subsumption is involved occurs when a subsumption is terminated. For example, consider the following story.

(10-11)   John and Mary were happily married for a number of years. Then one day, John was killed in a car accident.

The reader of story (10-11) must realize that John being killed terminates the marriage subsumption state for Mary. Being married normally subsumes a number of goals for the participants that must now be dealt with individually. For example, Mary might now be lonely, or have trouble paying the mortgage. She might therefore also desire to subsume these goals again. Thus a planner in this situation might look for a higher paying job as a way of subsuming her financial goals; similarly, a story understander would interpret such an action as a plan aimed at subsuming these needs.

In terms of my planning model, the termination of a subsumption state actually has no special significance. Rather, it is just an instance of a state being undone that was fulfilling some purposes, and those unfulfilled purposes now become active goals again. However, in terms of story understanding, such an event has a distinguished status. The termination of a subsumption state generally causes problems for the planner, and these tend to be the basis for interesting dramatic situations (see Wilensky, 1980, for a more detailed analysis of the role of goal relationships in the saliency of story components).

10.2.2.2 TYPES OF SUBSUMPTION STATES

Goal subsumption is a general principle that could be applicable to any recurring goal, regardless of its novelty. However, a number of particular subsumption states are important in their own right, if only because of their pervasiveness. I discuss some of these here mostly to illustrate the importance of this concept in everyday planning situations.

The following appear to be frequently occurring types of subsumption states:

1. Ownership of a Functional Object—Functional objects are objects that are normally used for particular plans. Thus the state of owning an object that has a function can subsume the goal for which that object is used. For example:

(10-12)   John decided to become a paid assassin. He bought a gun.

Assassin's frequently have to kill people. In order to make it easier to fulfill this goal each time it arises, John decided to subsume the recurring goal by acquiring ownership of a weapon. Once this state is realized, John can use the gun to murder his victims without having to deal with the "have weapon" precondition of this plan.

2. Streams—A *stream* is a continual source of a consumable substance. For example, having a job is an example of a social stream that supplies the employee with money. If a planner can establish some means of tapping a stream of some consumable resource, he can subsume those goals for which the consumable may be used. For example:

(10-13)   John was hungry because he lost his job.

Here an understander needs the knowledge that having a job can subsume goals requiring money to infer that the reason John was hungry was that he could no longer afford to buy food after his stream of money dried up.

3. Social Relationships—Being in a social relationship imposes a set of obligations upon a person. An obligation is a type of theme specifying how a person should act in particular situations. For example, being married implies that each person in the marriage relationship is obligated to help fulfill the other's emotional, sexual, and economic needs. Since social relationships tend to be relatively long term, the obligations they impose upon another person may serve to subsume a planner's goal. For example:

(10-14)   John was tired of working for a living. He quit his job and married a rich woman.

It is the subsumptive nature of marriage that explains the relation between John's goal and his attitude toward his job.

4. Knowing Some Fact—Another class of goal subsumption relationships has to do with committing a fact of to memory. For example:

(10-15)   When John became treasurer of the club, he memorized the combination to the safe.

To understand why John memorized the combination, the understander must realize that the goal of opening the safe is likely to recur for John, and that knowing the combination to the safe will make it easier to open the safe each time the need arises.

10.2.3   Plan Overlap

Situations can arise in which the execution of a single action fulfills a number of distinct goals simultaneously. For example, consider the following stories.

(10-16)   John had a crack on his wall. He decided to cover it with his favorite poster.
(10-17)   John decided he should be more physically fit. He was also something of a masochist, so he decided to take up jogging.
(10-18)   John wanted to go see the new disaster movie. He also wanted to see Mary, so he called her up and asked her if she'd go see the movie with him.

Each of these situations contains different goals that happen to be amenable to the same plans. For this reason, they are termed *plan overlap* situations. Most often, a plan that simultaneously fulfills a number of goals is a normal plan for one of these goals and just happens to fulfill another goal in a particular set of circumstances. Thus in story (10-16), putting up the poster is more properly a plan for displaying the poster than it is for covering a crack. I use the term *piggybacking* to refer to those plan overlap situations in which the use of the plan is normal for one goal but novel for the other.

When a plan overlap arises, the planner essentially assures that the same plan instance is associated with the overlapping goals. This requires merging the plans so as to preserve the maximum constraints on the individual plans. For example, in story (10-16), displaying the poster only requires that the poster is on the wall, whereas covering the crack constrains its location further. The single resulting plan, of course, must conform to the more severe constraints in order to apply to both goals.

When **DON'T WASTE RESOURCES** spots essentially identical plans, it creates the meta-goal *AVOID-REDUNDANT-PLANS*. This goal is fulfilled by the meta-plan *MERGE-PLANS*, which results in the creation of a single plan that preserves the constraints from each original plan. I elaborate on this meta-plan in the next section.

10.2.3.1   COMMON-SCHEMATA MERGING

In several instances it is possible and desirable to merge plans that are similar but not identical. For example, consider the following stories.

(10-19)   *John was going to go camping for a week. He went to the supermarket and bought a week's worth of groceries.*
(10-20)   *Johnny wanted a toy and a candy bar. He asked his father for enough money for both.*

In story (10-19), the planner is fulfilling several goals, each of whose plan has the prerequisite of having food. These plans are not identical because they each require buying different food tokens, namely, the food associated with each meal. However, to accomplish these plans efficiently, it is still desirable to merge these plans so that they all can be achieved by one instance of shopping at the supermarket. Similarly, in (10-20), getting each item requires money, but not the same money. A single instance of asking can still be used, provided that the total amount needed is requested.

This sort of merging is possible because these plans employ the same plan schema; only the parameters of the plan schema vary. Moreover, the parameters of the plan can be bound to indefinite lists rather than to a single item. In addition, the preconditions of the plans are not in conflict if both plans were to be executed simultaneously.

For example, buying different food items involves only the plan schema of shopping at the supermarket. This plan allows that an arbitrary number of items be purchased in a single execution. In addition, the same preconditions apply in each case. Thus any number of plans involving buying at the supermarket can be merged into a single plan simply by merging their parameters.

Note that this same merging process cannot go on if one of the specified criteria is not met. For example, buying a house and buying some food cannot be merged this way, as they do not share a common buying schema. If the schemata were identical, but the preconditions incompatible, the plans could not be merged. Thus buying items that could not be found at the same location could not be done in a single shopping plan because this would require the planner to be in different places at the same time.

To allow **MERGE-PLANS** to operate in these "common schemata" situations, it needs to be refined somewhat. First, it must check that the preconditions for the plans are compatible. This is easily enforced by making this a precondition of **MERGE-PLANS**. That is, **MERGE-PLANS** is given the precondition that the preconditions of the object plans be true simultaneously. This is verifiable by checking for goal conflicts.

Second, **MERGE-PLANS** employs a subplan called **MERGE-PARA-METERS**. **MERGE-PARAMETERS** combines the parameters of the individual plans into single parameters of the merged plan. If the parameters are identical or entail one another, a single parameter is used; otherwise, the parameters are appended into a list, provided that the plan in question supports such parameters.

Once **MERGE-PLANS** is so structured, "common schemata" situations become identical to plan overlap. We need only change the condition in which an

AVOID-REDUNDANT-PLANS meta-goal is detected to include situations in which common plan schemata arise. The case that corresponds to true plan overlap is now a degenerate instance in which preconditions and parameters are the same and in which *MERGE-PLANS* simply has an easier job.

As was mentioned earlier, a number of Sacedoti's general-purpose critics turn out to be particular instances of meta-plans for various meta-goals of the **DON'T WASTE RESOURCES** meta-theme. In addition to general-purpose critics, Sacerdoti postulates the use of "task-specific" critics. As an example, in a domain which requires the use of tools, he suggests the use of a tool-gathering critic that informs the planner to gather all the tools in a single trip to the tool box. In the formulation offered here, such task specific critics are not needed. Instead, the meta-plan *MERGE-PLANS* would constrain the task network to include only a single plan because of the presence of common plan schemata.

Even in Sacerdoti's framework, an additional general-purpose critic would appear to be preferable to a domain-specific one in this case, because the strategy is general to similarly structured domains. However, because of its specific commitment to separating domain knowledge from knowledge about planning, the meta-planning model is more conducive to the distillation of such general planning principles. In addition, the meta-planning model explains why one schedule is better than the other, whereas the critic-based model leaves the heuristic unmotivated.

10.2.3.2 PARTIAL PLAN MERGING

A situation related to plan overlap occurs when the execution of a plan for one goal makes it easier to fulfill another goal, but does not accomplish that goal outright. For example, consider the following stories:

(10-21)   *John needed some instant pudding. He decided to pick some up at the supermarket he passed on the way home from work.*

(10-22)   *John was shopping for a watch for himself. Then he noticed that the store was having a fabulous one cent sale, so he bought a watch for Mary as well.*

In both situations, the execution of one plan can lower the cost of another, although it does not replace the need for the other plan. If John stops at the supermarket as he passes it on the way home in story (10-21), he saves himself the driving that would normally be entailed by such a trip. However, his plan of driving home has to be extended to bring him to the supermarket, as the original plan would not have done so. Similarly, in story (10-22), the price of the second watch is greatly reduced once the plan for the first one is decided on, but an additional buying event must still be scheduled (perhaps to be merged with the first) in order to fulfill a goal of having the second watch.

These examples are cases in which plans partially overlap, and in which savings are realized through scheduling. That is, in each case, a single action can be made to contribute somewhat to more than one goal; thus a benefit can be realized by scheduling these plans together so that the common part need not be duplicated. For example, in story (10-21), part of the driving can be beneficial to both goals. Therefore it is important to schedule the plans for these two goals together so that an extra trip is not needed. In story (10-22), the situation is similar in that the purchase of the first item contributes to the purchase of the second, if the purchases are done simultaneously.

To secure maximum advantage requires trying the various permutations of plan ordering, and this of course can be computationally expensive when the number of plans involved is large. However, some heuristics are useful in eliminating obviously defective plans. For example, if a plan schedule contains a step that involves undoing or retracing a previous step, an attempt should be made to try another schedule. This is the case in story (10-21), where going home first would entail an extra trip to the store and back. Occasionally, information about the efficacy of a particular schedule may be available. This is true in (10-22), as the mention of the one cent sale is equivalent to stating that a cost reduction is incurred by executing two plans simultaneously.

In terms of meta-planning, this means that **DON'T WASTE RESOURCES** will detect a meta-goal called *ACHIEVE-OPTIMUM-SCHEDULE* in response to a number of situations, including those just described. The meta-plan associated with this goal is called *SCHEDULE-PLANS-TOGETHER*. This plan will try to find a schedule that minimizes the total cost by considering plans together. Thus, in story (10-21), getting the milk will be scheduled just before going home, because this provides the minimum expenditure; in story (10-22), the plans are scheduled to be simultaneous.

Note that binding plans together in a schedule may effect plan selection in complicated ways. For example, if two plans involving traveling are bound together, a common means of transportation will have to be used. If this is not already the case, the current plan structure may have to be revised.

The meta-plan *SCHEDULE-PLANS-TOGETHER* may be thought of as a way of doing a plan merge in which the entire contents of the plans are not mergable. Instead, the plans are partially merged so that the common content of both plans can be most effectively utilized.

10.3 GOAL CONCORD

Positive goal interactions may occur between the goals of different individuals as well as among the goals of a single individual. Consider the following stories.

(10-23)   *John wanted to get ride of Fred. He hired Bill as a hit man, and gave him a gun.*

(10-24)   *John and Bill were partners playing golf. Bill hit a shot into the rough. John sneakily moved the ball into a better position.*

A situation in which the goals of different planners that are mutually beneficial to one another is called *goal concord*. In story (10-23), John enlists Bill as his agent, causing him to share the same goal. In story (10-24), John and Bill share each other's goal because each is dependent on the other's goal being fulfilled for the success of his own goal.

Within one individual, goals can overlap because either the goals themselves have an intrinsic similarity (mutual inclusion), or because different goals can be achieved by similar plans (plan overlap). In the case of concordant goals across individuals, only the first situation properly arises. That is, two individuals may have essentially identical goals, but they cannot really have identical plans. This is because plans are of the form "planner will perform some action." Since the planners will be different, these plans are not obviously mergable. However, it is quite likely in such cases that the planners share identical goals or subgoals and that they can take advantage of a concordant relationship between these goals.

For example, if two planners both happen to have the plan of going from San Francisco to New York, an appropriate plan cannot be proposed on this basis alone—if in both cases the goals dominating these plans are to be in New York to propose marriage to Mary, it is unlikely that any concordance should be recognized. On the other hand, if the dominating goals are to deliver a couple of packages, and if the two planners have a cordial relationship, a more efficient plan may be worked out.

Although plan overlap does not occur between the goals of different planners, some issues related to goal concord do not arise in goal overlap. For example, the two preceding examples differ in whether one of the planners caused the other to have the concordant goal. The next two sections treat each possibility.

10.3.1 Mutual Inclusion of Different Planners' Goals

To have concordant goals, two planners must have essentialy the same goal state. As is the case for goal overlap, the two goals need only entail one another, rather than be identical, for an inclusion relationship to exist. If the origin of the goals is independent, an applicable strategy is to form an *alliance*. An alliance is a joint commitment to a goal or to a task network stemming from that goal. Forming an alliance combines the resources and abilities of both planners so that they may be able to execute plans that each would otherwise not be able to accomplish, or could only accomplish with great difficulty and less certainty. For example, consider the following story.

(10-25)   *The United States and China were afraid of the Soviet Union, so they signed a mutual defense pact.*

Here both the US and China have an anticipated preservation goal of protecting itself from the Soviet Union. Thus they decided to take a common action against the Soviet Union if the need should arise.

Pooling resources and abilities provides the planners with more options than individual plans since there are basic limitations on individuals that do not apply to groups. For example, consider the following story.

(10-26)   John and Mary were hungry. Mary went to buy some wine while John cooked dinner.

As an alliance, John and Mary are not bound by the limitations of one individual's ability. Thus they are able to execute these plans simultaneously.

In addition, the existence of concordant goals can affect plan selection. For example, consider this story.

(10-27)   Everyone in the village faced a water shortage during the dry season. They decided to pitch in together and build a reservoir.

Here the cost of one plan is too prohibitive for an individual planner. However, since a large number of planners would benefit from this project, pooling their resources enables this plan to be adopted on the basis of cost-effectiveness.

In terms of meta-planning, the relevant meta-theme in these situations is again **DON'T WASTE RESOURCES**. This theme causes an *AVOID-REDUN-DANT-GOALS* meta-goal to be created when a concordant goal is detected. *AVOID-REDUNDANT-GOALS* is the same meta-goal used in goal overlap to prevent a planner from achieving the same goal twice. There it is subject to a meta-plan that makes sure that the same instance of the goal is tied to all the relevant plans in the planner's task network. Here, the applicable meta-plan is called *POOL-AND-COORDINATE*. This meta-plan requires that the planners involved come to an agreement on a joint plan of action, which may involve pooling resources and allocating individuals to specific subtasks. In this way, each planner is saved the cost of achieving each of those goals on its own.

As story (10-27) indicates, *POOL-AND-COORDINATE* may require the selection of a plan that is inappropriate for an individual planner. That is, part of agreeing on a joint plan of action requires the individual planners to propose joint plans that may be quite different from ones they would propose for themselves alone. This can be done by considering plans that require more resources than could be considered by individual planners. In addition, the coordination aspect of *POOL-AND-COORDINATE* entails the complex problem of dealing with other planners. Thus an attempt to apply this plan by a set of planners is apt to involve the use of many planning structures designed specifically for communication and coordination tasks.

Another strategy applicable here is actually quite general. *AVOID-REDUNDANT-GOALS* should be activated if a planner anticipates that a desired state will come true in the future of its own accord. The applicable meta-plan is to schedule no action for this goal. We may call this meta-plan *WAIT*. That is, the resultant behavior would be for the planner to wait for the goal state to come true, and then proceed with the rest of the task network.

Applied to goal concord, this strategy would suggest waiting when another planner is expected to carry out one's goal on its own. In principle, neither *WAIT* nor *POOL-AND-COORDINATE* can be preferred over one another. This question is resolved by applying the full goal calculus to see which alternative maximizes expected value. For example, if one planner thought the other fully capable of achieving the goal alone, and if the first planner had no additional goal of helping the other, the preferred strategy is to wait. If on the other hand the planner thought that the other planner would fail alone, or if the first planner were driven by a theme such as fairness, a cooperative strategy would prevail.

As is the case for goal competition, goal concord does not really constitute part of the basic structure of plans. This is because each planner is driven by its own goals, the goals of other planners only having an effect by virtue of their influence on the planner's own goal structure. Thus goal concord strategies are not preferred for any principled reason other than that they may help an individual planner's prospects for fulfilling its own goals.

Alliances may also be motivated by other meta-themes. For example, a planner can increase the chances of success by pooling resources with another agent. In this case, the operative meta-theme is **ACHIEVE AS MANY GOALS AS POSSIBLE**, which would be triggered by the pending failure of one of one's goals. In the case where a concordant goal is already in existence, these cases are identical to other forms of goal concord just described. When a planner with a concordant goal is not to be found this may lead to a form of goal induction.

10.3.2 Goal Induction

Sometimes a planner may induce a goal in another, thereby causing the other to have a concordant goal. Consider the following story.

(10-28)   *Nixon hired Colson to head his dirty tricks team. Colson decided to bug the Democratic party's headquarters.*

Nixon's agent assumes Nixon's goal of continuing the Nixon presidency. Since undermining a rival will contribute to this goal, Colson's action in (10-28) is comprehensible.

Employing an agent is a planning strategy that is useful for overcoming the limitations imposed by an individual's time and abilities, and when there does not already exist another planner with a concordant goal. Thus employing an agent will be motivated by the meta-theme **ACHIEVE AS MANY GOALS AS POSSIBLE**, as the situations that motivate its use are those in which some goal is in danger of failing due to the limitation of a planner's abilities. For example, employing an agent can be used to resolve goal conflicts, such as those based on time shortages, or to prevent failure of a goal that requires a plan involving a skill not possessed by the planner.

In addition, unlike independent goal concord, once an agent has been employed, there is generally a well-understood division of labor, namely, the agent assumes responsibility for the accomplishment of the assigned goal. Thus **EMPLOY-AGENT** is a meta-plan applicable to a number of planning problems resulting from the limitations of an agent, rather than a true goal concord situation. That is, the plans applicable to goal concord do not apply here, because the division of labor is already decided. This situation merely superficially resembles goal concord because, once an agent is employed, the employer will want the agent's goals to be accomplished. However, this is merely because the agent's goals are equivalent to the goals the planner would have had if he had opted to execute the plan himself.

10.4 SUMMARY

The existence of overlapping and concordant goals may enable a planner to produce a more efficient means of fulfilling its goals. In the case of goal overlap, the planner can avoid redundant steps by collapsing similar goals and plans or by establishing subsumption states for a recurring goal. When a planner's goal is found to be in concordance with the goals of other planners, the planner may reduce costs and increase the chances of success by letting other planners do part of the work.

11

Computer

Implementation—Representation

of Task Networks

11.1 INTRODUCTION

This chapter motivates and describes the representations used in two computer programs that implement the theories of understanding and of plannng. PAM (Plan Applier Mechanism) is a story understanding program based on the model of explanatory reasoning described in the initial chapters of this book. PANDORA (Plan ANalysis with Dynamic Organization, Revision, and Application) is a plan generation program that incorporates the model of planning. The control structure of these systems and examples of their processing capabilities are illustrated in Chapter 12.

11.2 IMPLEMENTATION AND METHODOLOGY

Throughout this book I have argued that a large and complexly interacting set of goals underlies many actions. This is certainly the case for building computer systems. Both scientific and practical goals are involved. As scientific tools, computer implementations can show the feasibility of a theory by successfully emulating the behavior the theory is aimed at explaining. Such implementations can also demonstrate the problems with a theory, manifest by a program's inability to function correctly or as anticipated. Perhaps most importantly, computer implementations can highlight whole new problem areas. Previously these problems may have been entirely unforeseen or only dimly understood. In addition, attempts to build a working system can shift a researcher's focus by demonstrating forcibly the importance of some problem area or the limited role of a commonly pursued direction of research.

   Computer implementations also have as their goal the automation of some useful task, such as text understanding or autonomous planning. While the goal of such work does not necessarily involve building a system that fulfills a pressing need, such considerations do motivate the design of our systems, and even affect the nature of the scientific theories produced in important ways.

The interplay between scientific and pragmatic considerations deserves further mention. For example, many of the ideas presented in this book came out of specific problems with previous program implementations, which I will discuss. Thus problems related to facilitating implementations structured the search for theoretical entities, and moreover structured the shape that the theories took. Implementation difficulties led to key questions that might not have been asked otherwise, and therefore contributed to the scientific understanding of these problems.

However, the fact that implementation is a useful strategy for theory testing and development does not mean that it is without its methodological problems. Two of the most important of these are the following. First, it is often difficult to make an attribution about what is wrong with a program. For example, an implementation may not work as the theory predicts because it is a poor implementation, or because the theory is inadequate. If the programs implemented were simple, it might be a straightforward matter to answer this question, just as it may be possible to examine experimental equipment or to have a different group of researchers run an experiment again. Unfortunately even ''simple'' computer programs are quite complex objects, and AI programs are among the most complicated programs written. Generally, only the person most responsible for a program really has any grasp on what may be wrong with that program, and researchers rarely have the resources or motivation to rewrite experimental systems. Thus the analysis of what went wrong is most often left to a single individual.

Programs generally do not either work or not work, but exhibit some in-between behavior that is difficult to describe. For example, the program may work fine on several examples, but be extremely difficult to extend to another. Or it may be that the extention to another example can be done only at the cost of the program's ability to process a case that it could previously handle. Since these sorts of problems are usually problems of the interaction between program components, it is difficult to attribute them to specific theoretical deficiencies. Another example of this problem is the division of a program into a control structure and a set of data structures. How the division is made may significantly affect the assessment of a problem. For example, embodying something in a process that would best be represented delaratively may cause a deficiency in one's representational system to appear as a problem in one's control structure. The latter may be diagnosed as an implementation defect rather than as a theoretical problem, although one's theory is actually at fault.

A second problem with this methodology is that the tasks that AI researchers are interested in implementing go beyond the particular theory being developed. For example, the theory of explanatory inference described in the preceding chapters is useful for building a natural language understanding system. But a large number of other theories is needed as well, such as theories about the extraction and representation of the meaning of linguistic utterances, the storage of these representations in memory, question answering, summarization, and paraphrase.

Thus modules based on a large number of theories are required to produce a working system. When a problem arises it is difficult to know which module is really at fault, or if the fault is in the interaction between modules. More importantly, a researcher is not likely to have a theory of all the aspects of a task, and of necessity will develop some modules to a lesser extent than others. This makes it even harder to put the blame on a particular attribute of the theory in which one is most interested; problems can always be attributed to the less well understood domains.

For my own part, I believe that efforts to deal with these methodological problems have themselves been beneficial theoretically. For example, these problems led me to try to build systems whose structure is as clear as possible, both so that theoretical problems would be more apparent, and so that the systems would be extensible. This forces the theories to take a certain form from which the questions upon which this book is based are the obvious questions to ask. Thus, so far, implementation goals and theoretical goals appear to be overlapping rather than in conflict.

11.3 PREVIOUS VERSIONS OF PAM AND THEIR PROBLEMS

Both the theories of planning and of understanding have undergone several implementations, which are still in a state of flux. In particular, the initial versions of PAM, which were implemented considerably before the initial versions of PANDORA, were based on a set of representations quite unlike those currently in favor. This is because these previous versions contained a number of problems that gave impetus to much of the theory discussed in this book. The repercussions of these problems influenced not only the theory of understanding, but the theory of plans, and thereby the theory of planning as well. Thus understanding the nature of these problems is useful for understanding the current implementation and its underlying goals. Although many of the examples of PAM input/output that follow demonstrate an older version of the program, that implementation will be described here primarily to highlight its deficiencies. A more detailed account of this particular implementation is described in Wilensky (1980) and in Schank and Riesbeck (1981).

11.3.1 Request-Based Systems

The original version of PAM is based on a concept called the *request* (Riesbeck, 1975). Requests are essentially production rules (Newell and Simon, 1972) whose activation is dynamic. A production rule is a condition-action pair, the action of which is executed when the condition it describes is matched. Such condition-action pairs encode the knowledge that the system possesses. Unlike standard production systems, in which the conditions of all productions are tested periodically, not all requests are so tested. Rather, only a small set of "active" requests have this distinction. In addition, one of the effects of the execution of a request may be to cause other requests to be activated or deactivated. Thus contextual effects are manifest in a request-based system by controlling the set of requests that are active at any one time.

The action that a request normally carries out is to build a structure. Typically this structure would be used to fill in some unfilled "slot" in another structure. For example, original PAM (hereafter referred to as O-PAM) has a request that becomes active when a goal is discerned. This request states, roughly, that each incoming concept be examined to see if it is a plan applicable to this goal. If so, the action part of this request adds that plan into a structure associating that plan with the goal. This structure represents the belief that this plan is a plan for some particular goal. Once this is done, the request "self-destructs," as one no longer wants to examine input for something already found.

In general, all requests trying to fill a slot are removed once that slot has been filled. Several different requests might be competing to fill a slot, all of which would be removed after one of them succeeds. However, only the request that succeeds would cause more requests to be activated, that is, added to the list of requests whose conditions PAM inspects. Thus the request that asserts that some particular plan is aimed at some particular goal might also cause a request to be activated that looks for a certain condition signaling the success of that plan; another request might look for signs of its failure.

Request-based systems are essential goal-directed in that empty slots in a structure represent "needs," and a request attached to a slot is an attempt to fulfill such a need. This allows independent knowledge sources to simultaneously suggest various ways to carry out a task. Once the task has been completed (i.e., a request has filled in a slot), all efforts aimed at fulfilling this need can be conveniently terminated simply by removing the requests associated with that slot. In addition, requests represent small pieces of knowledge, and thus the program can manipulate pieces of knowledge independently of one another, provided that the requests can be formulated so that they do not explicitly refer to one another. In theory, the programmer should be able to increase the knowledge of the system simply by adding another request, and without having to drastically alter other components of the system.

11.3.2 Problems

Programming with requests has many of the problems generally associated with production systems, plus a few of its own. For example, since requests work by filling slots in structures, it is generally necessary to have a structure available beforehand that has all the appropriate slots in it. Thus, to associate a plan with a goal, a kind of plan-goal association structure needs to exist that asserts this relationship. Since either the plan or goal is likely to be known before the other, upon seeing one, a structure must be created that holds an empty slot for the other. In the preceding example, upon seeing a goal, O-PAM must create an object with a place for a goal and a place for a plan, in order to have a place in the future to attach the plan when it is seen. This situation is illustrated in Fig. 11.1.

In Figure 11.1, the large box represents the plan-goal structure needed to hold a place for an unknown plan, given a known goal. The slots for the plan and goal are represented by the smaller boxes within this structure. The goal slot in the figure is already filled with some content, but the plan slot is empty, waiting to be filled by a request labeled R1. This request is shown scanning the input for a suitable plan. Should one be spotted, it would be used to fill the plan slot. (In actuality, the request must scan not only the input, but inferences made from the input, since an explanation may require several steps.) Note that this structure must be created as soon as the goal is encountered in order to provide a place to which a request might be attached.

There are several problems wth this idea. First, it requires that structures exist in anticipation of some need for them. Thus, in Figure 11.1, the plan/goal structure must be created upon learning of the goal, even though there is as yet no plan to associate with it. Often this sort of anticipation is wasteful because it may create structures that are never referenced again. Sometimes it is just not feasible. For example, if a story involves a succession of goals, a structure must exist from the beginning anticipating such a succession, or else any relationship between the goals is difficult to represent. The typical way this problem is resolved in O-PAM is

A Structure Necessitated by Requests   Figure 11.1

PLAN/GOAL Association Structure

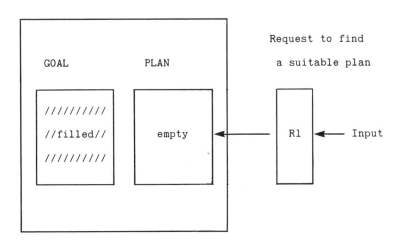

by creating some ad hoc structure to contain all contingencies, or if this is not possible, by using some mechanism outside of the usual request facility. The result of this is both the frequent creation of fairly meaningless but necessary structures just in case some relationship is detected later on, and a set of behind-the-scenes mechanisms that handle the cases not treatable in this manner.

Goal conflict and goal competition are cases in point. Upon hearing a goal, one does not always expect to hear of a conflicting or competing one. Therefore, one would like not to have to prepare for these contingencies in advance, but still be able to denote them when they arise. However, since requests work by filling in slots in structures, it is difficult to denote a goal conflict when one is detected unless there is a previously prepared slot into which an assertion designating the conflict is to be put.

In general, the relations between all sorts of entities in a representation of a story are complex, and it is not possible to anticipate them all. Also, because there may be many relationships between the same components, some more network-like representation is required. Requests tend to be better for tree-like structures in which a node is generally filled in with a structure, but are poor for denoting complex relations that cannot be represented in acyclic graphs.

Another problem with request- or production-based systems is that they make it difficult to capture certain important generalizations. For example, O-PAM embodied the idea that a goal can be explained by finding a plan for which that goal fulfills a precondition. Unfortunately this idea is only expressed implicitly by the particular set of requests that are activated when various concepts are encountered. That is, the request that adds a plan to the representation has to activate a request looking for goals aimed at fulfilling that plan's preconditions. One such request must be associated with each particular plan. Thus the same fact has to be duplicated for each plan known to the system. The same defect holds for many other situations, resulting in a proliferation of requests.

Another problem with production systems is that they promote procedural encoding of knowledge. That is, the system's knowledge is embodied in the fact that a particular production will execute some action in a particular situation or, in the case of requests, activate other requests as well. As is the case with the previous example, this tends to prevent the same piece of knowledge from entering into different computations. For example, I discussed the desirability of using the same knowledge for both understanding and planning. However, facts such as ''State S is a precondition for Action A'' need not be represented explicitly in production systems, but can be encoded as part of the rule whose purpose is to use that fact in understanding. In particular, this fact could be part of a request that tried to associate an incoming plan with a previously known goal.

Of course, in these cases, it is possible to build a production rule that internally consulted a declarative knowledge base of plan-goal associations. However, doing so in a sense circumvents much of the idea of a production system. Also, since it is not really necessary to do so, production systems generally do not encourage the programmer to provide such an articulate rendition of his or her theory as a declarative discipline would require. Moreover, some flow of control is generally encoded in productions, either by specifying requests to activate or by having productions create states used only to trigger the activation of other productions. Knowledge encoded in this fashion will be useless to anyone not explicitly interested in using those productions for one particular purpose.

Problems with procedural encoding of knowledge are manifest in other ways. For example, consider the case of goal conflict detection. (This represented a theoretical difficulty as well for O-PAM, because detecting a goal conflict falls outside the simple explanation paradigm and a separate goal conflict detection mechanism is required. The introduction of meta-planning alleviates this difficulty.) Upon learning of a goal, O-PAM needs to activate a request that states "if another goal is detected, check to see if it is in conflict with this one, and if so, represent the conflict and load requests looking for resolution, etc." Since O-PAM does not know in advance which goal it will encounter first, such a request must be attached to all goals.

This not only entails redundancy, but complicates processing considerably, as routines associated with each item must be prevented from interfering with one another. In the case of goals, for example, each will be trying to detect a goal conflict with the other, and we want to be sure that one, and not two, goal conflict is detected. This latter problem is an instance of a kind of timing problem that pervades production-like systems and is a cause for much of the complexities that these programs manifest.

Having redundant requests leads to runtime inefficiencies as well. In general, each element added to the story representation causes a set of requests to become active. The conditions of these requests must now be examined at each iteration. However, since requests come and go dynamically, and since their conditions are arbitrary, these conditions cannot be checked in some clever way, for example, by indexing them. This results in a runtime search through a linear list of requests to decide which ones are triggered. Processing is thereby slowed down considerably as the number of items encountered (and thereby the number of active requests) increases during the course of story understanding. As was indicated, it is often necessary to have redundant requests, so the slowdown may be more than is justified by the number of additional items in the story representation.

Part of this problem stems from two facts about request-based systems. First, they make it difficult at times to easily express the processing generalization I wish to enforce. Second, they require the attachment of knowledge to individual items (in this case, goals) that is really knowledge about the interactions of these items (i.e., goal conflicts). Thus it is desirable to be able to express known generalizations conveniently, to index them according to the kind of objects to which they refer, and to prevent indexing and processing details from constraining what we want to represent.

11.4 PEARL

As the preceding remarks indicate, previous implementations of PAM did not clearly reflect the theory PAM was supposed to implement. In addition, since much of the knowledge was encoded procedurally, it would be difficult to share this knowledge with other programs, such as a plan generation mechanism. Also, it was difficult to represent complex relationships between objects represented in memory, and it was often necessary to introduce special purpose processes, for example, for goal conflict detection. PAM was slower than it might be, because active requests cannot be indexed efficiently and are often redundant.

To overcome these problems, we devised a representation AI programming language called PEARL (Package for Efficient Access to Representation in LISP). PEARL was implemented by Michael Deering and Joseph Faletti (Deering, Faletti, and Wilensky, 1982). PEARL is similar in some ways to other representation languages, such as KRL (Bobrow and Winograd, 1977) and FRL (Roberts and Goldstein, 1977). However, PEARL combines features of these frame-like languages with more predicate calculus oriented representations, and in this way somewhat resembles PROLOG (Roussel, 1975). PEARL encourages the user to express facts declaratively, and discourages (but permits) procedural attachment. However, PEARL does not commit itself to any particular theory of representation or inference. That is, it does not automatically do theorem proving nor does it require users to classify entities into a number of theoretically important categories.

PEARL is more constrained in scope than other knowledge representation languages, combining a number of useful features into a very efficient package. In part, this is because we want PEARL users to exploit the features we understand; other representation languages provide so many features and options that it is often difficult to understand where the power of the system comes from. In part it is because the system is under development, and we want to see what features are really needed rather than being all things to all people from the outset. We also wanted PEARL to be efficient, and efficiency is often inversely proportional to complexity.

PEARL allows the user to define types of structures, to make individuals and patterns of those types, and to store and fetch these objects in associative data bases. In addition, the user may easily specify information about how these objects are likely to be accessed, and PEARL will use this information to set up transparent and efficient retrieval structures. PEARL also supports an inheritance scheme so that information about classes of objects can be represented efficiently. Similarly, default values for slots can be specified for classes of object; these would automatically be used to fill a slot upon creation if no filler is then specified.

Both the initial versions of PANDORA, written by Joe Faletti (Faletti, 1982) and the newest version of PAM, written by Peter Norvig, are implemented in PEARL. As an example of its benefits, the version of PAM written in PEARL runs about ten times as fast as the request-based version on comparable hardware. To describe PEARL's other benefits, we first give a brief description of PEARL, next show how various kinds of knowledge can be represented, and then describe a PAM implementation in PEARL.

11.4.1 PEARL Structures

PEARL structures consist of predictates with labeled slots. In this manner, they resemble the format for frames used by Charniak (1978). For example, the user can define a goal-type object to consist of the predicate Goal, followed by a Planner slot to be filled by a representation for the possesser of the goal, and an Objective slot to be filled by a representation of the target state. Thus a generic goal has the form:

(Goal (Planner. . .) (Objective. . .))

For this discussion, I will not present the syntax through which one actually defines and manipulates such structures, as it involves complexities whose introduction is not otherwise warranted. A detailed account of PEARL may be found in Deering, Faletti, and Wilensky (1982).

To represent the particular fact that John has the goal of having some book, for example, the following structure is used:

(Goal (Planner John1)
(Objective (Poss (Actor John 1)
(Object Book1))))

Here John1 and Book1 denote individual objects that presumably have been defined elsewhere; Poss is a predicate indicating possession, which itself takes slots for the Actor who possesses and for the Object possessed.

Patterns in PEARL look just like structures, but the slots are filled with variables. For example, a pattern that matches any goal of a person possessing an object would have the following form:

(Goal (Planner ?Who)
(Objective (Poss (Actor ?Who)
(Object ?Obj))))

Using the standard AI convention, pattern variables are spelled with an initial question mark. Since the Planner slot of the Goal predicate and the Actor slot of the

Poss predicate use the same variable, this pattern will only match objects in which these slots have identical fillers.

Patterns have a number of purposes in PEARL. They can be used to determine whether some object is of a particular sort, and they can be used to query a data base for objects matching a specific structure. In addition, patterns can be stored in the data base, in which case they represent general facts. For example, suppose we wished to represent the fact that having an object is necessary in order to use that object. This could be represented in PEARL as follows:

(Precondition
*   (Action (Use (Actor ?Planner) (Object ?Object)))*
*   (State (Poss (Actor ?Planner) (Object ?Object))))*

That is, for any planner to use any object, that planner must possess that object. Thus pattern variables in objects in a data base serve the same function as universally scoped quantifiers in predicate calculus formulas.

Other preconditions for a particular action would be stated as additional individual predications. In general, a PEARL data base will be composed of a large number of individual structures like these. The data base may be fairly permanent, in which case it will probably encode knowledge such as the fact used in the preceding example, or it may be a temporary data base, in which case it is likely to contain a story representation consisting of specific events, states, and relationships that become known during the course of understanding a story.

When a PEARL data base has been built up (through explicit insertions by a user program), items may be fetched from that data base by specifying patterns to the fetcher. For example, if a user wished to know what goals John has, a pattern of the following form could be given to the fetching mechanism:

(Goal (Planner John1) (Objective ?0))

This would match all objects in the data base conforming to this structure. PEARL returns these objects in a stream, or virtual list. That is, the actual result of a fetch is a complex structure. The user requests successive items in this structure by passing it through a "next-item" function. This is done to prevent the costly retrieval of long lists when the first few elements of a list will suffice.

The elements fetched in this fashion may contain pattern variables as well. For example, to determine all the preconditions for using a particular object, say, a knife, a fetch could be done using the following pattern:

(Precondition
*   (Action (Use (Actor ?Planner) (Object ?X Knife)))*
*   (State ?X))*

Here the third item in the Object slot of the Use predicate is a constraint. This particular constraint will cause a match to fail if the corresponding Object filler is not of the type "knife." The result of a fetch using this pattern would be a stream of Precondition formulas containing the known precondition for the use of a knife.

Constraints are implemented using routines that are accessed during matching. That is, Knife runs a particular routine that determines whether something is a knife. As such, this feature of PEARL is a concession to procedural attachment. In theory, it is possible to replace these procedures with PEARL structures. for example, one can add the predication (Knife ?X), and force ?X to refer to the same ?X as the preceding predication. Although we are in fact moving toward such representations, in practice, it has been more convenient to allow this breach of declarative structure, and trust the implementor not to abuse it by adding constraints that would not otherwise be expressible or which perform some complex computation.

Again, in practice, it is more likely that the information contained in the preceding example would be stored in the form of preconditions of more specific actions, such as cutting, rather than under something as general as Use. PEARL allows for the expression of relationships, such as that between using a knife and cutting with a knife, as well as mechanisms for transparently retrieving such information upon different sorts of requests. This is done using a fairly standard inheritence mechanism that will not be elaborated on here.

As mentioned, PEARL allows for the efficient indexing of these structures. For example, if the user knows that Precondition formulas will be retrieved using the predicate filling the Action slot as a key, but not using that filling the State slot (this is the case in the preceding example, he can specify this fact and PEARL will index such facts accordingly. Multiple indexing is permissible. In general, PEARL retrieves facts very rapidly, thus encouraging users to make liberal use of its data base facilities in their programs. Using a test data base of 4000 entries, PEARL takes an average of only about 4.2 CPU milliseconds for an unsuccessful query, and 7.3 CPU milliseconds for a successful query on a PDP KL-10. (PEARL also runs on the VAX11, on which most of the program development described here is now taking place.)

11.4.2 Representing Task Networks in PEARL

The representation of a story in PAM or a plan in PANDORA consists of a large number of individual PEARL assertions. These assertions express events, states, goals, objects, time information, and relationships between such items. Since these items are indexed so that they can be retrieved through assertions that relate them, the entire set of propositions representing a story can be thought of us a large network. However, unlike conventional semantic networks, the links from one item to another are not automatic. Rather, these are determined by the particular relationships asserted and the indexing structures used.

The most commonly used representations in a PAM story understanding session or a PANDORA planning session are those for actions, goals, and relationships between these items. The vocabulary for action representations is based on Schank's Conceptual Dependency Theory (Schank, 1975). However, the programs use a set of complex actions as well as primitive ones to represent activities. For example, the primitive Ptrans is used by Schank to represent actions which change the location of an object. In PEARL, the sentence "John went home" is represented as follows:

```
(Ptrans P1
    (Actor John1) (Object John1) (To Loc1) (From NILSYM))
(Residence (Actor John1) (Place Loc1))
(Person (Actor John1))
(Male (Actor John1))
(Firstname (Actor John1) (String John))
(Location (Object Loc1))
```

The first expression states that John transported himself from some unknown place to some location; the second, that this location is John's home. The remaining predications express other properties of the objects John1 and Loc1. PEARL allows us to associate identifiers with assertions, such as the P1 contained in the Ptrans predication. Other predications can be made about this particular Ptrans by referring to this identifier. However, unless such identifiers are needed, they will be omitted here.

These are shorthand representations conveying several different kinds of facts. For example, the Ptrans is shorthand for denoting that P1 is an instantiation of a Ptrans frame, that John1 is in the Actor relation to this instantiation, that Loc1 is in the To relation to it, and so on. Similarly, the Person predication denotes that John1 instantiates the person frame; it does not specify relations to this frame, such as Firstname, which are given separately. On the other hand, the Residence predication denotes a simple relation between the objects denoted by John1 and Loc1.

In the examples that follow, objects like Loc1 will be used without the accompanying defining expressions such as (Location (Object Loc1)). Such expressions are required for PEARL to function properly, but they are cumbersome and should be easily inferred by the reader.

Nonprimitive actions are represented by a similar notation. However, the predicates of these actions are further described by other assertions. For example, John driving a car somewhere might be described by the expression:

```
(Drive-vehicle
    (Driver John1) (To Loc1) (From Loc2) (Vehicle Car1))
```

Drive-vehicle will have been defined as being a kind of Ptrans, so this relationship is implicit in this representation. In addition, the internal structure of the concept is available through an Expansion predication. This would be of the following form:

```
(Expansion
    (Item (Drive-vehicle
        (Driver ?X) (To ?TL) (From ?FL) (Vehicle ?V)))
    (Subparts DV1 DV2...)
    (Relations...))
```

An Expansion is really a pointer to a set of predications that exist separately in the data base. These predications describe the set of actions that constitute the complex item, as well as relationships between these actions. For example, Drive-vehicle would include the facts that the driver starts the engine and then puts the vehicle in gear. Each of these facts would be a PEARL expression. In addition, the fact that the first event precedes the second would be another separate assertion.

The individual components of Drive-vehicle are not shown in the preceding example for several reasons. First, they constitute a large set of items. They also use some special PEARL facilities so that the individual predications can share variables. Moreover, the detailed nature of these interrelationships is the subject of another theory not described herein, and which is not particularly relevant to this discussion.

PAM and PANDORA enclose events inside predicates indicating various mental states to show that they are intentions rather than actions. When these occur, the specific occurrence is also asserted, and an Intention-to-Action predicate is used to relate the plan to the actual event. Other than this, the representation of plans and actions is identical.

Other important structures in PAM and PANDORA are Goal, Precondition, and PlanFor. Examples of the first two have been given in the previous section. PlanFor associates an action with a goal and has the following form:

```
(PlanFor
  (Goal...) (Action...))
```

For example, to assert that driving is a way of getting somewhere, the following PEARL notation is used:

```
(PlanFor
  (Goal
    (Goal
    (Planner ?X) (Objective (At (Actor ?X) (Location ?L))))
  (Action
    (Drive-vehicle
      (Driver ?X) (To ?L) (Vehicle ?V)))))
```

That is, for a planner to get himself to a location, he can drive a vehicle to that location.

The programs use a Result predicate to link an action to its results. For example, the fact that both the driver and the vehicle end up at the place driven to is represented as follows:

```
(Result
  (Action
    (Drive-vehicle
      (Driver ?X) (To ?L) (From ?FL) (Vehicle ?V)))
  (State
    (At (Actor ?X) (Location ?L))))
(Result
  (Action
    (Drive-vehicle
      (Driver ?X) (To ?L) (From ?FL) (Vehicle ?V)))
  (State
    (At (Actor ?V) (Location ?L))))
```

Since driving has been asserted to be a kind of Ptrans, the fact about the location of the driver will probably not be included. Rather, this would be implicit in the inheritance structure, because the more general fact that this is true for Ptrans most likely has been inserted.

In general, both PAM and PANDORA maintain relations inferred between components. For example, when PAM is processing a story and uses a fact such as one of these to establish the connection between two items, an instantiated version of the fact is added to the representation, along with the two items. Thus if PAM learned that John came to be in L.A. because he drove there, a Result predication would be added along with the action and state to indicate the connection between them. That is, the following three propositions will be asserted into the data base:

```
(Drive-vehicle Event1
    (Driver John1) (To L1) (From NILSYM) (Vehicle NILSYM))
(At State1 (Actor John1) (Location L1))
(Result
    (Action Event1) (State State1))
```

In this example, PEARL creates the objects Event1 and State1, an action and a state, respectively. Then the Result predicate can be made to refer to these particular items by referencing these objects.

Goal relationships are stored via explicit predicates, such as ConflictingGoals and CompetingGoals. Goal subsumption is a bit more elaborate because it requires slots for the subsumed goal, the plan through which subsumption is to be carried out, the precondition to fulfill, and the state that fulfills it.

The predicate Normal is used to express that some fact is the normative one. For example, to express that people normally want money, the following notation is used:

```
(Normal
    (Concept
        (Goal (Planner ?X Person)
            (Objective (Poss (Actor ?X)
                (Object ?0 Money))))))
```

In general, PEARL does not have elaborate mechanisms for dealing with quantification, so the semantics of statements such as this one are determined largely by how they are interpreted. Also, a number of other predicates are used to represent a multiple of states and physical objects, and story-related entities such as *points* (Wilensky, 1980). As these are not particularly relevant here, I omit the actual representations used.

The main point of this exposition is to give some idea of how the basic elements of the theory can be denoted. No doubt, the representations shown here are incomplete, and we will continue to refine them. As mentioned earlier, nothing in the theory commits us to this particular representational scheme. However, the scheme so far has proven to be reasonably extensible and conducive to efficient programming, while maintaining the declarative bias inherent in the theory.

12

Computer
Implementation—Programs

12.1   INTRODUCTION

This chapter describes recent implementations of PAM and PANDORA, which use the PEARL representations introduced in the previous chapter. Examples of program input/output are given to illustrate the status of these systems. Although both programs are experimental systems, PAM in particular is a program that is more likely to continue to be extended rather than redesigned. Additional facilities beyond the theories discussed earlier have already been added. PANDORA, on the other hand, is far newer, and fewer claims are made for it. It would not be surprising if better implementations were subsequently created. However, because many of the changes in the development of PAM have already been incorporated in PANDORA, it is likely that these changes will be less sweeping than the changes PAM has already undergone.

12.2   FAUSTUS—An Implementation PAM In PEARL

The examples given in Chapter 11 show how facts, events, and task network elements are represented in PEARL for use in planning or understanding. Much of the explanation algorithm described in Chapter 5 can also be represented explicitly in PEARL. This is done by expressing facts pertaining to explanation as causal frames, indexed under the item caused. These frames can then be used in accordance with some general principles of frame manipulation, which, when applied to these causal frames, produce an explanation.

A recent frame-based implementation of PAM, called FAUSTUS (Frame Activated Unified Story Understanding System), has been implemented by Peter Norvig. When an input occurs, FAUSTUS looks for frames indexed under that input. FAUSTUS then looks for confirming or refuting evidence for these frames. Positive evidence generally consists of additional references to the same frame; negative evidence consists of direct negations of frame constituents or evidence for a frame known to exclude the frame in question. Frames whose status cannot be immediately resolved are kept about for further evaluation. Causal frames that connect an input to a story representation constitute an explanation of that input. Some of the frames have slots that will be filled only by subsequent events; such future occurrences will provide confirming evidence for those frames' relevance.

For example, learning that someone is hungry will invoke the frame that hunger leads to the goal of satisfying hunger. If it is not already known that the person has this goal, invoking the frame in effect predicts it. If, later on, this same frame is suggested by some other evidence, such as a hypothesis generated to explain an action of going to a restaurant, then the goal can be inferred.

This particular example illustrates a forward inference process, in which knowledge is used for predictive rather than explanatory purposes. During the explanation process, FAUSTUS checks predicted frames before consulting memory, so that predictions both shorten and bias the search process. In effect, explanation finding is just a particular application of the more general process of frame recognition and verification. Various kinds of frames are associated with concepts, including other frames, and frames for which there is sufficient evidence are inferred as being true. An explanation is just a set of causal frames which are inferred because each is sufficiently supported by its association with other frames.

FAUSTUS constructs explanations and performs other frame-based processes by using the following frame manipulation primitives:

1. Invocation—Initially considering a frame. Frames are currently invoked because they have been indexed under a component that occurs as an input, or because they are explicitly associated with another invoked frame.

2. Determination—Deciding if enough evidence for an invoked frame exists to infer the frame.

3. Instantiation—Creating an instance of a determined frame to represent its occurrence on a story.

4. Elaboration—Filling in an empty slot of an instantiated frame. This process corresponds to the top-down processing performed extensively by systems like SAM and Ms. Malaprop.

5. Termination—Realizing that an instantiated frame is no longer relevant.

6. Attrition—Allowing an invoked but undermined frame to fade from subsequence consideration. FAUSTUS measures time in terms of the number of frame invocations that have passed. Thus, if enough new frames are invoked before a previously invoked frame is determined, FAUSTUS will drop that frame from subsequent consideration.

These primitives are used to effect a number of design principles of FAUSTUS as an intelligent system. To see how they implement explanation, consider the following example. An explanation for a goal is that it fulfills a precondition for some planned action. This may be expressed in a PEARL frame as follows:

```
(Leaderto
    (Causer((Intend (Planner ?P) (Action ?A))
            (Precondition (Action ?A) (State ?O))
            (Not (Concept ?O))))
    (Caused (Goal (Planner ?P) (Objective ?O))))
```

That is, a goal can arise if a planner intends to perform some action, and if that action requires an unmet precondition to be met. Thus to explain a goal, check to see if the planner has an intended action for which achieving the goal will fulfill a precondition. If so, this fact constitutes an explanation for the input. (Actually, expressing multiple concepts in a PEARL slot is somewhat more awkward than the example would indicate. I ignore this complication in this discussion.)

FAUSTUS uses such facts as follows. When FAUSTUS has an input, it first looks at instantiated frames to see if the input elaborates one of them, and then looks for frames that are indexed under the input. Causal frames such as the preceding one will be invoked by this process. Some of the invoked frames may be marked as mutually excluding one another. FAUSTUS's determination process then looks for verification of these frames. Supporting evidence includes the previous mention of one of these frames or of their constituents. Thus FAUSTUS checks the story representation and other invoked frames for corroborating items.

For example, to apply the fact just given, FAUSTUS would check to see if it already has any intended actions in its story representation data base. If some are found, FAUSTUS continues by checking the next Causer conjunct, thereby asking if the goal would achieve a precondition for one of these actions and, finally, if the precondition is unmet. If so, this frame will be determined; other invoked frames marked as being mutually exclusive with this one will be removed from the invoked list.

Of course, facts confirming propositions like the preceding Precondition clause would be found only in permanent memory. Note that since all the variables in this clause will have been bound prior to this fetch, FAUSTUS will merely be asking permanent memory for verification of a particular fact at this stage.

If an explanatory frame is not determined by this procedure, FAUSTUS allows invocation to spread along the constituents of invoked frames. In the preceding example, spreading invocation along the Precondition clause of the invoked Leadto, with variable ?O bound but variable ?A unbound, results in a set of new invoked frames. For example, if the Objective of the Goal denoted John being at a particular restaurant, and stored in the permanent data base is the fact that being at a restaurant is a precondition for eating at one, this stage would invoke eating at that restaurant as a candidate action. In effect, FAUSTUS will have hypothesized the explanation that John intended to eat at the particular restaurant he wanted to be at.

All the frames invoked in this manner are now subject to confirmation. If one can be determined, the others will be either eliminated by exclusion or removed soon by attrition. If not, invocation will spread out again from the invoked frames. In this manner, FAUSTUS implements the contextual effects described in Chapter 5. That is, if a reasonable explanation can be found within the story, it will be. (A long, tenuous explanation may not be found due to attrition). If not, then intermediate hypothesizes are suggested until a connection with the story can be found.

Since these explanation facts are just ordinary PEARL structures, they are kept in the data base and fetched according to the input. Since PEARL's indexing allows such retrieval to be fast, this mechanism is relatively efficient. Inefficiency results primarily when multiple frames are associated with a frame and when explanation chains are long. In practice, the branching factor has been small (usually one and occasionally two or three) and the chains relatively short (7 was the longest) for well-formed stories. Of course, a system with more knowledge might cause these numbers to be increased.

Two aspects of explanation that are conceptually a bit different from this are thematic explanations and explanations involving normalcy. These are where the explanation process ultimately stops. However, they are implemented through the mechanism just described. In the case of themes, these specify as a cause some state that should exist. This state is generally marked as Normal and will be assumed on the next iteration. Things that are stored as Normal are found to be true in the permanent data base and thus cause immediate determination.

The following additional frames are used in FAUSTUS's explanation algorithm:

```
; An explanation for a goal is a theme.
(Leadto
   (Causer ?Theme)
   (Caused (Goal (Planner ?P) (Objective ?O))))
```

Use of this fact results in a check of permanent memory for situations that can give rise to the goal. Evidence for the existence of such a situation is then sought.

```
; An explanation for an action is a plan.
(Leadto
   (Causer (Intend (Planner ?Actor) (Action ?Input)))
   (Caused (Action (Actor ?Actor))))
```

Here FAUSTUS relies on the fact that the input is bound to ?Input in order to have bindings for both the actor and the entire action. Since ?Actor will always be bound to the actor of the input, during spreading invocation, this fact will only invoke the frame denoting that the actor intended this action.

```
; An explanation for a plan is a goal.
(Leadto
   (Causer ((Goal (Planner ?P) (Objective ?O))
            (Planfor (Result ?O) (Method ?A))))
   (Caused (Intend (Planner ?P) (Action ?A))))
; An explanation for an action is that it is part of another action.
(Leadto
   (Causer (Substep (Action ?E) (Subpart ?A)))
   (Caused ?A Action))
```

This fact encodes the hierarchical explanation that an action will be planned because it is part of a more complex action already planned. In general, this step will cause another action to be inferred that will be recognized as a plan for some goal.

```
; A short-circuited explanation for an input is that it is normal.
(Normal (Concept ?Input))
```

12.2.1 Text Comprehension Principles

The preceding exposition describes how FAUSTUS's explanation algorithm is implemented in terms of frame manipulation. As has been mentioned, FAUS-TUS's frame manipulation is designed to conform to a set of text comprehension principles, of which computing an explanation is just an instance. These principles, which may be viewed as implicit goals of the understanding process, include the following:

1. The Principle of Coherence—Determine those frames that provide a coherent construal of the inputs.

2. The Principle of Concretion—Determine as specific a frame as is possible from an input. This is derived from the First Law of Knowledge Application, which instructs us always to employ the most specific applicable knowledge.

3. The Principle of Least Commitment—Make only the minimal assumptions necessary to determine a frame (This was suggested by Marr 1977).

4. The Principle of Exhaustion—Determine enough frames to account for all of the input.

5. The Principle of Parsimony—Determine those frames that maximize connections between inputs (suggested independently by Granger 1980 and by Fillmore and Kay in Kay 1982).

6. The Principle of Poignancy—Determine the point of what is being said.

The Principle of Coherence motivates the finding of explanations. Specifically, FAUSTUS is driven to find an explanation by the policy of spreading invocation further along Precondition, Planfor, and other explanation-related structures than along non-explanation-related structures.

The Parsimony Principle accounts for the fact that in sentences like "The chef went down to the wharf and bought some fish from a fisherman" the reader infers that the chef bought the fish for use in his restaurant from a fisherman who caught it (The example is taken from Kay 1982). These inferences are made because, in accordance with the Principle of Parsimony, they allow the additional connections of fisherman frame and chef frame with the buying frame. The Principle of Exhaustion insures that these frames are considered, because it requires frames to be invoked that are associated with each component of the input.

Frame manipulation is similarly used to determine story points. Points are represented as rather abstract frames to which certain affective importance is attached. For example, a subsumption state terminating and thereby creating a problem for a planner is usually an interesting story fragment. The frame representing this abstract event (i.e., a subsumption state terminating and leading to a problem) is indexed by its subsumption state termination slot, causing the termination of a subsumption state to invoke the frame. As with any other invoked frame, this frame may be determined if enough evidence can be found. For example, subsequent mention of a resulting difficulty may determine the frame as it elaborates one of its slot. The resulting determined, elaborated frame, along with other such abstract frames, constitutes the point structure of the story.

The Principle of Concretion instructs the system to find the most specific frame that matches the input. For example, if FAUSTUS learns that John loves Mary, it needs to realize that this is romantic love rather than sibling love in order to make accurate predications about John's behavior. Thus a form of inference is required in which semantic knowledge from the sentence (e.g., that some sort of love relation exists) is compared against pragmatic knowledge of relationship types (i.e., the various kinds of love), to find the interpretation that the speaker most likely intends.

FAUSTUS performs concretion as part of its general frame recognition process. That is, frames are associated with other frames that denote specialized versions of those frames, and FAUSTUS tries to decide among alternatives. The Principle of Least Commitment is also of use here. For example, in the case of John loving Mary, both romantic love and sibling love are suggested equally by the input. However, the former is inferred because the latter requires an additional assumption, namely, that John and Mary are brother and sister. In addition, frames can have different initial activations, so a default can be chosen from among frames supported by equal evidence. Choosing a default is thus derived from the Principle of Least Commitment, as a default is a normative value and therefore constitutes the minimal assumption one can make.

12.2.2 Some PAM Examples

The following are examples of actual PAM input/output. However, they were not all done using the same version of PAM. In addition, the different versions run in conjunction with a number of different related programs. The old version of PAM, written by this author, used ELI (Riesbeck, 1975) to parse English sentences into Conceptual Dependency; its output used a question answerer written by Janet Kolodner and an experimental English generation program written by Rod McGuire and Richard Granger. More recent versions, including one implemented by Michael Deering and Peter Norvig's FAUSTUS implementation, use the PHRAN natural language analyzer, written by Yigal Arens, as its front end, and the PHRED generation system, written by Steve Upstill and Paul Jacobs, for output (see Wilensky and Arens, 1980). The most recent versions have been used to process stories of considerable length, and contain other mechanisms beyond the ones discussed here. The most important of these is a mechanism for distinguishing important parts of a story from unimportant component.

The first set of stories demonstrates some general features of the understanding process.

INPUT TEXT:
> *Ann got into her car.*
> *She went for a drive.*
> *She arrived at the movie theater.*
> *She got a ticket.*

INPUT: *Why did Ann get a ticket?*
OUTPUT: *She wanted to see the movie.*

INPUT TEXT:
        Ann got into her car.
        She went for a drive.
        She got a ticket.

INPUT: *Why did Ann get a ticket?*
OUTPUT: *She violated a traffic law.*

In both these stories, the input "she got a ticket." is analyzed by PHRAN into the following PEARL representation:

(Atrans (Actor nilsym) (To Ann1) (Object Ticket1))

In the first version of the story, buying a ticket is one of the steps of the "movie-going" frame, and thus the input is incorporated into this frame, which was previously activated by a reference to going to the movie theater. That is, the input is considered to be an elaboration of the "ticket-buying" subframe of "movie-going." No other interpretation of the input is considered.

In the second version, getting a ticket is not found to be part of any activated frame. Indexing on this input returns a number of frames, including "traffic-violation" and "movie-going." Since traffic violation is related to the driving frame, it is chosen; the other unrelated alternatives are discarded. Thus concretion is performed on the input by finding the most precise frame consistent with the input that is supported by evidence from the story.

Most of the explanations constructed for these stories involve forward inferencing. For example, the explanation for getting into the car is that it fulfills a precondition for driving; the explanation for driving that it fulfilled a precondition for seeing the movie. In each case, explanations for events are enabled by subsequent inputs. The following stories demonstrate some additional forms of inference.

INPUT TEXT:
        John wanted money.
        He got a gun and walked into a liquor store.
        He told the owner he wanted some money.
        The owner gave John the money and John left.

INPUT: *Why did John get a gun?*
OUTPUT: *Because John wanted to rob the liquor store.*

INPUT: *Why did John threaten the shopkeeper?*
OUTPUT: *Because John needed to get some money.*

INPUT: *Why did the shopkeeper give John the money?*
OUTPUT: *Because the shopkeeper didn't want to get hurt.*

INPUT: *Why did John leave?*
OUTPUT: *Because John didn't want to get caught.*

OUTPUT:
STORY FROM JOHN'S POINT OF VIEW:

    I needed to get some dough. So I got myself this gun, and I walked down to the liquor store. I told the shopkeeper that if he didn't let me have the money then I would shoot him. So he handed it over. Then I left.

OUTPUT:
STORY FROM THE OWNER'S POINT OF VIEW:

    I was minding the store when a man entered. He threatened me with a gun and demanded all the cash receipts. Well, I didn't want to get hurt, so I gave him the money. Then he escaped.

INPUT TEXT:

    Willa was hungry.
    She picked up the Michelin Guide and got into her car.

INPUT: *Why did Willa pick up the Michelin Guide?*
OUPUT: *Because Willa wanted to know where a restaurant was.*

INPUT: *Why did Willa get into her car?*
OUTPUT: *Because Willa wanted to get to a restaurant.*

INPUT: *What were the consequences of Willa picking up the Michelin Guide?*
OUTPUT: *This enabled Willa to read the Michelin Guide.*

OUTPUT:
THE STORY FROM WILLA's POINT OF VIEW:

    I wanted to get something to eat, but I didn't know where a restaurant was. So I picked up the Michelin Guide, and I got into my car.

INPUT TEXT:

    John wanted Bill's bicycle.
    He went over to Bill
    and asked him if he would give it to him.
    Bill refused.
    John told Bill he would give him five dollars for it,
    but Bill would not agree.
    Then John told Bill he would break his arm
    if he didn't let him have it.
    Bill gave him the bicycle.

INPUT: *Why did John walk over to Bill?*
OUTPUT: *Because he wanted to get his bicycle.*

INPUT: *Why did Bill give his bicycle to John?*
OUTPUT: *Because he didn't want to get hurt.*

INPUT: *What were the consequences of John's walking over to Bill?*
OUTPUT: *This enabled him to ask him to give him Bill's bicycle.*

INPUT: *What were the consequences of John's asking Bill to give him Bill's bicycle?*
OUTPUT: *Bill told him that Bill wouldn't give him Bill's bicycle.*

OUTPUT:
THE STORY FROM JOHN'S POINT OF VIEW:

    I wanted to get Bill's bicycle. So I walked over to him, and I asked him to hand it over. He told me that he wouldn't hand it over. So I asked him to sell it to me for five dollars. Then he told me that he wouldn't hand over his bicycle. I told him that if he didn't hand it over then I would break his arm. He handed over his bicycle.

THE STORY FROM BILL'S POINT OF VIEW:
> *John came over. He asked me to give him my bicycle. I wanted to keep the bicycle, so I told him that I wouldn't give it to him. Then he offered to buy it for five bucks. I wanted to keep the bicycle, so I told him that I wouldn't give it to him. He told me that if I didn't give it to him then he would break my arm. I didn't want to get hurt. So I gave him my bicycle.*

The next set of stories demonstrates the processing of various goal relationships by PAM.

Goal Subsumption:
INPUT TEXT:
> *John and Mary were married.*
> *Then one day, John was killed in a car accident.*
> *Mary had to get a job.*

INPUT: *Why did Mary need employment?*
OUTPUT: *John died and so she needed a source of money.*

In the preceding example, PAM infers that John's death terminates a subsumption state for Mary, and that she may seek to replace it. PAM uses this inference to infer that the explanation behind Mary's goal of getting a job.

Goal Conflict:
INPUT TEXT:
> *John wanted to watch the football game,*
> *but he had a paper due the next day.*
> *John watched the football game.*
> *John failed Civics.*

INPUT: *Why did John fail a course in Civics?*
OUTPUT: *He failed to hand in an assignment.*

Here the example shows an inference based on knowledge about goal abandonment. Namely, that watching television precluded John from fulfilling his other goal of handing in a paper, and thus this goal led to his failing the course.

INPUT TEXTS:
> *Wilma wanted to have an abortion.*
> *Wilma was Catholic.*
> *Wilma converted from Catholicism to Episcopalianism.*

> *Wilma wanted to have an abortion.*
> *Wilma was Catholic.*
> *Wilma went to an adoption agency.*

> *Fred wanted to take his gun hunting.*
> *Fred wanted Wilma to have a gun at home.*
> *Fred only had one gun.*
> *Fred bought another gun.*

INPUT TEXT:
> *Daryl hopped into his car.*
> *He was late for work.*
> *Then he noticed there were a lot of cops around,*
> *so he decided to stick to the speed limit.*

In the first two stories, PAM detects a conflict beween Wilma's goal of having an abortion and her inferred goal of not having an abortion because she is Catholic. In the first story, PAM infers that Wilma resolved the conflict by changing the circumstance that gives rise to one of her goals, and fulfilled the other (i.e., she decided to have the abortion). In the next case, PAM infers that Wilma abandoned her goal of having an abortion because it meant less to her than violating her religious beliefs. The third story is a goal conflict based on a resource shortage. Here PAM infers that Fred bought another gun so he could take one with him and leave one at home. Finally, in the last story, PAM detects a conflict between getting to work on time and getting a ticket; this is used to determine that Daryl felt that avoiding the ticket was more important than getting to work on time.

Goal Competition:
INPUT TEXT:
> *John wanted to win the stockcar race.*
> *Bill also wanted to win the stockcar race.*
> *Before the race, John cut Bill's ignition wire.*

INPUT: *Why did John break an ignition wire?*
OUTPUT: *Because he was trying to prevent Bill from racing.*

This story contains an instance of a goal competition situation involving anti-planning. PAM explains John's action as part of a plan to undermine Bill's efforts by undoing a precondition for Bill's plan.

The following example demonstrates a number of features of PAM together, including its ability to determine the poignant parts of stories. This is reflected in the associated summary.

INPUT TEXT:
> *John graduated college. John looked for a job.*
> *The Xenon Corporation gave John a job. John was*
> *well liked by the Xenon Corporation. John was*
> *promoted to an important position.*
> *John got into an argument with John's boss.*
> *John's boss gave John's job to John's assistant.*
> *John couldn't find a job. John couldn't make*
> *a payment on his car and had to give up his car.*
> *John also couldn't make a payment on his house,*
> *and had to sell his house, and move to a small*
> *apartment.*
> *John saw a hit and run accident. A man was hurt.*
> *John dialed 911. The man's life was saved. The*
> *man was extremely wealthy, and rewarded John with*
> *a million dollars. John was overjoyed. John bought*
> *a huge mansion and an expensive car, and lived*
> *happily ever after.*

PHRED STORY SUMMARY:
> *John worked for the Xenon Corporation.*
> *The Xenon Corporation fired John.*
> *John could not pay for his house and his car.*

John was broke.
A man gave John some money.
John was rich.
John got a new car and a new house.

Note that this summary is flawed, as it neglects to include the important fact that John saved the rich man's life. This is due to a bug that had not been corrected at this time, although it represents no theoretical difficulty.

12.3 PANDORA

A prototypical version of PANDORA has been implemented by Joe Faletti using PEARL. This program currently functions in two domains. One is a domain of mundane activities, such as going outside to get the morning paper, in which PANDORA acts as an autonomous agent. The other is the more specialized domain of the UNIX* operating system. In this domain, PANDORA acts as part of the UC (UNIX Consultant) natural language interface to UNIX (Wilensky, 1982).

PANDORA is being made to function over these two domains for several reasons. As the theory of plans was developed primarily from the consideration of mundane situations, selecting some such domain was *de rigueur*. However, I was also interested in testing the hypothesis that much of what is generally termed "expert reasoning" is actually just the application of common-sense reasoning applied to a more esoteric domain. If PANDORA were properly constructed, it should function in a more technical domain simply by the addition of domain-specific knowledge. In addition, providing a technical expert would be a useful application of these ideas.

UC is a system that integrates natural language understanding with planning and problem solving to provide a painless interface to an operating system for the naive user. The intent behind UC is to help the user learn how to use the computer, rather than become the mainstream user-interface. The assumption is that a user will prefer natural language when first confronted with an unfamiliar system, but will eventually prefer a less verbose, if more cryptic, formal language once he becomes well versed in it.

UC works by first using PHRAN to analyze a user's request into its meaning, represented by PEARL structures. The request then passes through a *goal analysis* module whose function is to determine the intent behind the user's request. This inferred intention is then passed to PANDORA, which tried to compute a plan to fulfill it. Computing this plan involves accessing a PEARL knowledge base of facts about UNIX, with which UC has been equipped. Since UC is largely concerned with tutoring users, and requests are most often requests for information, UC will most often use this plan to formulate a response to the user. The response is then passed to PHRED, which expresses it in English.

---

*UNIX is a trademark of Bell Laboratories.

The goal analysis module, though not part of PANDORA, is relevant to some of the issues we have discussed. This module uses knowledge about goal structures to infer the actual goal behind a user utterance. The goal analyzer is responsible for making well-known speech act-type analyses (Perrault, Allen, and Cohen, 1978), such as determining that statements of needs are requests for action. This would be used to translate inputs like "I need more disk space" into the goal of obtaining more disk space, which can then be passed to PANDORA.

In addition, the goal analyzer often needs to infer goals even when a goal is stated. For example, consider the question, "How can I prevent someone from reading my file?" A superficial analysis of this input would yield the goal "prevent someone from reading my file," and this would be sufficient for formulating the response of changing the file's protection. However, an additional option is avilable in UNIX, namely, encrypting one's file so that it would appear to be jibberish to someone not in possession of the key used to encode it. The problem here is that this does not literally prevent someone from reading the file, but merely from understanding its contents when it is read. Thus the original request would not cause this response to be retrieved.

The solution used here is to equip the goal analyzer with knowledge of normative goals. For example, preventing someone from reading a file would not be listed as normative, but preventing someone from learning the contents of a file would be. The goal analyzer, in trying to construe the input as a normative goal, tries a number of heuristics, one of which is to interpret an input as a misstatement of a problem. In this case, the input would be construed as a too narrow statement of the known normative goal, and this normative goal would be passed to PANDORA for processing.

Much of the interpretation of a request in UC is done by PANDORA. In particular, PANDORA must do goal detection and deal with goal interactions in order to provide the user with reasonable responses. For example, suppose UC were asked the question, "How can I get more disk space?" A problem here is to prevent the generation of the response, "Delete all your files," which would satisfy the literal request. To prevent such a response, UC must detect a preservation goal if it first proposes this plan, because its execution will remove some files desired by the user. Then PANDORA must infer a goal conflict between these two goals. A resolution to this conflict, for example, obtaining more of the scarce resource, would result in a more reasonable plan, such as asking the systems manager for a large quota.

As PAM and PANDORA share much of their planning knowledge, much of the representational machinery just described applies to PANDORA as well. PANDORA must deal with three kinds of objects: events, plans, and goals. Its overall structure consists of a simple loop that considers these objects as follows:

    1. Process External Events—If one exists, process it. This generally involves the Noticer and the Goal Detector, as well as an inference system.

    2. Plan for Goals—If there are no external events to deal with, plans are selected for unplanned goals. The Plan Selector and Projector are brought into play here.

3. Plan Execution—If no goals remain to plan for, the plan at the top of the plan queue is executed.

To reason about the consequence of various events, states, and plans, PAN-DORA uses a knowledge base of frame-like structures and associates these structures with the more salient of their constituents. Thus PANDORA and PAM share a great deal of frame manipulation machinery. For example, to determine the consequences of it raining, PANDORA stores a fact like:

```
(Leadto
    (Causer ((At (Object ?Person Person)
                (Location Outside))
            (Weather (Object Outside)
                (Condition Raining))
            (Not
            (State (Wearing (Person ?Person)
                            (Object ?Gear RainGear))))))
    (Caused (Dryness (Object ?Person)
                (Degree Neg))))
```

This fact states that a person outside in the rain without protection will get wet. The fact is indexed under (Weather (Object Outside) (Condition Raining)), but it could be indexed under its other constituents as well. Thus when PANDORA learns that it is raining, this item will be fetched. Then PANDORA checks to see if any other of the item's premises are true. New facts are also examined to see if they relate to a premise. When all the conditions in a premise are true, the conclusion can also be asserted.

This mechanism is used for goal detection. That is, a goal is one of the things whose cause may be described by such a frame. In many cases, there is only a single premise, so a goal can be asserted right away. For example, the item

```
(Leadto
    (Causer (TimeOfDay (Time Morning)))
    (Caused (Goal (Objective
                    (Know (Object (State (Object World)))
                        (Knower Ego)))
            (Planner Ego)))
```

denotes the fact that, in the morning, the planner wants to find out what is happening in the world. Thus when PANDORA learns that it is morning, it asserts the fact that it has the goal of finding out what is going on.

If there are no more events to process, PANDORA tries to find a plan for this goal. It does this by first checking for known normal plans for this goal. One such normal plan for this goal is the following:

```
((NormalPlanfor
    (Result (Know (Object (State (Object World)))
                (Knower Ego))
    (Method ((Ptrans (Actor Ego) (Object Ego) (To Outside))
            (Grasp (Actor Ego) (Object Newspaper))
            (Ptrans (Actor Ego) (Object Ego) (To Inside))
            (Read (Actor Ego) (MObject (State (Object World)))
                (From Newspaper)))))
```

That is, to find out what is going on in the world, go outside, pick up the newspaper, bring it inside, and read it.

The next step is to simulate the plan. To do this, consequences of the executing a plan are asserted into a hypothetical data base instead of the ordinary data base of beliefs. Simulating going outside will add to such a data base the fact that the planner is outside. PANDORA checks each such assertion in a manner similar to that just described. That is, it checks to see if it has any relevant frames available to draw new conclusions. Having previously learned that it is raining, the preceding item adds a premise to this frame. PANDORA operates under the "closed world" hypothesis, assuming what it does not know is false, so it believes that it is not wearing a raincoat. Thus PANDORA concludes that it is wet. However, since this is happening during simulation, the conclusion is placed in the hypothetical data base.

As this conclusion is added, PANDORA again checks its knowledge base for relevant items. In this case, it finds the following item:

```
(Leadto
   (Causer (Dryness (Object ?Person) (Degree -5)))
   (Caused (Goal
              (Objective (Dryness (Object ?Person)
                                   (Degree O))
              (Planner ?Person))))
```

That is, a person who is wet will want to become dry. Since this is happening in the simulation, the goal becomes a preservation goal.

Thus this goal gets asserted into the data base of facts and the process is iterated. This time, the following piece of knowledge is accessed:

```
(Leadto
   (Causer (Cause (Causer ?Plan EgoPlan))
                  (Caused ?Goal PreservationGoal)))
   (Caused (Goal
              (Objective (Resolve-Conflict
                          (Task1 ?Goal)
                          (Task2 ?Plan)))
              (Planner ?Person))))
```

That is, if a plan caused the planner to have a preservation goal, assert the meta-goal of resolving the conflict. (Determining that this Cause is true is currently done by the interpreter, which must check to see how the goal arose. This is a problem with the current implementation.)

The method retrieved for this goal is the following:

```
(NormalPlanFor
   (Result (ResolveGoalConflict
            (Task1 ?T1)
            (Task2 ?T2)))
   (Method (FindNormalPlan
            (Situation ((?T1 ?T2))))))
```

This method is to try to find a stored plan for both tasks. At this point, there is nothing else to do, so PANDORA begins plan execution. This meta-plan is on top of the queue, so it is tried first. Executing it results in a search for a plan for situations involving going outside and preserving dryness, and the following stored plan is retrieved:

```
(NormalPlanFor
    (Result ((Dryness (Object ?Person) (DegreeO))
            (Ptrans (Actor ?Person) (Object ?Person) (To Outside))
            (Weather (Object Outside)
                    (Condition Raining)))
    (Method ((PutOn (Actor ?Person) (Object Raincoat))
            (Ptrans (Actor ?Person) (Object ?Person) (To Outside)))))
```

This states that a plan for going outside and keeping dry is to wear a raincoat. Note that this requires using **MAKE-ATTRIBUTION** on the plan of getting the newspaper to determine that going outside while it is raining is what is salient. This general routine is not implemented; the preceding instance is handled by a special case rule in the interpreter, another deficiency in the current implementation.

The plan finally produced is to put on a raincoat, and then go outside, pick up the paper, bring it inside, and read it. Unfortunately, as of this writing, PANDORA will read the paper standing in its raincoat, dripping on the rug.

Another example of PANDORA is from the UC domain. UC itself can handle a wide variety of English requests for information about UNIX. The following dialogue illustrates some such simple interactions in which PANDORA is not largely involved:

User: How can I delete a file?
UC: typing 'rm filename' will remove the file with name filename from your current directory
User: move a file?
UC: typing 'mv filename newfilename' will move the file with name filename to a file with name newfilename
User: How might a file be created in UNIX?
UC: the best way to create a new file is to use the editor, i.e. - 'vi filename'
User: a directory?
UC: typing 'mkdir dirname' will create the directory 'dirname' in the current directory
User: How can I find out how full the disk is?
UC: typing 'df' will tell you how full the disk is
User: How can I find out who is on the system?
UC: typing 'who' will tell you who is connected to UNIX
User: How do I print a file on the line printer?
UC: typing 'lpr filename' will print the file filename on the line printer
User: What is a search path?
UC: A search path is a list of directions in which the operating system searches for programs you have asked it to execute.

An example that involves PANDORA occurs when an action fails because of insufficient disk space. As of this writing, this example does not work in conjunction with the English interface. That is, in this example, PANDORA believes that it, rather than the user, is having a problem, and plans to solve it for itself. Insofar as the planning is concerned, there is little difference. However, I generated the following English dialog from the plan structure PANDORA creates.

In this example, PANDORA believes it is trying to write out a file it has been editing, but gets a message that it has run out of disk space.

User: I have run out of disk space writing out a file in vi.
UC: Try deleting unneeded files.
; Here PANDORA determined that a conflict exists between
; maintaining current files and writing out the new file.
; It tries to resolve it first by trying to reclaim some
; of the resource consumed by continuous enablement.
User: I still don't have enough space.
UC: Mail the file to yourself.
*   Then ask the systems manager for*
*   more disk space.*
; The original plan fails, so PANDORA must try again.
; PANDORA replans by looking for a plan for the goal
; that doesn't require any disk space.
; Mailing to itself is stored as such a plan.
; In addition, PANDORA asks the systems manager for some more
; disk space in order to establish a goal subsumption state,
; because it knows that requests involving disk space are likely
; to recur.

After learning that the original plan fails, PANDORA first proposes to write the file in /usr/tmp, as all users may write in this directory, and thus this plan meets the computed constraints. This plan is discarded, however, because any user could subsequently destroy the file. That is, PANDORA predicts the eventual failure of the goal of saving the file using this plan, and thus the plan is rejected. An additional attempt to select an applicable plan results in the more satisfactory solution of making the file to oneself.

Bibliography

Bibliography

Abelson, R.P. (1973). The structure of belief systems. In R. C. Schank and K. M. Colby (eds.), *Computer Models of Thought and Language*. Freeman, San Francisco.

Abelson, R. P. (1975). Concepts for representing mundane reality in plans. In D. Bobrow and A. Collins (eds.), *Representation and Understanding: Studies in Cognitive Science*. Academic Press, New York.

Barr. A. (1977). Meta-knowledge and memory. Stanford University Heuristic Programming Project HPP-77-37 (working paper).

Barstow, D. (1977). A knowledge-based system for automatic program construction. In *Proceedings of the Fifth International Joint Conference on Artificial Intelligence*. Cambridge, Mass.

Berliner, H. J. (1974). Chess as problem solving: The development of a tactics analyzer. Ph. D. dissertation, Computer Science Department, Carnegie-Mellon University.

Bobrow, D. G., and Collins, A., editors. (1975). *Representation and Understanding: Studies in Cognitive Science*. Academic Press, New York.

Bobrow, D. G., and Winograd, T. (1977). An overview of KRL, A knowledge representation language. *Cognitive Science*. Vol. 1, No. 1.

Bruce, B. (1978). Plans and social actions. In R. Spiro, B. Bruce, and W. Brewer (eds.), *Theoretical Issues in Reading Comprehension*. Lawrence Erlbaum Associates. Hillsdale, N. J.

Carbonell, J. G. Jr. (1978). POLITICS: Automated ideological reasoning. *Cognitive Science* Vol. 2, No. 1.

Carbonell, J. G. Jr. (1979). Subjective understanding: Computer models of belief systems. Yale University Department of Computer Science Research Report #150.

Charniak, E. (1972). towards a model of children's story comprehension. AI TR-266, MIT.

Charniak, E. (1978). On the use of framed knowledge in language comprehension. *Artificial Intelligence*. Vol. II, No. 3.

Charniak, E. (1981). A common representation for problem solving and language comprehension information. *Artificial Intelligence.* (forthcoming).

Cullingford, R. E. (1978). Script application: Computer understanding of newspaper stories. Yale University Computer Science Research Report #116.

Davis, E. (1981). Organizing spatial knowledge. Yale University Computer Science Research Report #193.

Davis, R. (1977). Interactive transfer of expertise: Acquistion of new inference rules. In *Proceedings of the Fifth International Joint Conference on Artificial Intelligence.* Cambridge, Mass.

Davis, R., and Buchanan, B. G. (1977). Meta-level knowledge: Overview and applications. In *Proceedings of the Fifth International Joint Conference on Artificial Intelligence.* Cambridge, Mass.

Davis, R., and King, J. (1975). An overview of production systems. AI Memo AIM -271, Department of Computer Science, Stanford University.

Deering, M., Faletti, J., and Wilensky, R. (1982). Using the PEARL AI Package. Berkeley Electronic Research Laboratory Memorandum No. UCB/ERL/M82/19.

Dreyfus, H. (1972). *What Computers Can't Do; A Critique of Artificial Reason.* New York: Harper Row.

Duda, R. O., Hart, P. E., Nilsson, N. J., Sutherland, G. L., (1978). Semantic network representation in rule-based inference systems. In D. A. Waterman and F. Hayes-Roth, (eds.), *Pattern-directed Inference Systems.* Academic Press, New York.

Faletti, J. (1982). PANDORA—A program for doing commonsense planning in complex situations. *Proceedings of the Second Annual National Conference on Artificial Intelligence.* Pittsburgh.

Fikes, R. E., and Nilsson, N. J., (1971). STRIPS: A new approach to the application of theorem proving to problem solving. *Artificial Intelligence,* Vol. 2, No. 3-4, pp. 189–208.

Granger, R. (1980). When expectation fails: Toward a self-correcting inference system. *Proceedings of the first Annual National Conference on Artificial Intelligence.* Stanford, Calif.

Hayes-Roth, B., and Hayes-Roth, R. (1979). A cognitive model of planning. *Cognitive Science.* Vol. 3, No. 4.

Hewitt, C. (1970). PLANNER: A language for manipulating models and proving theorems in a robot. Research Report AI 168, Massachusetts Institute of Technology.

Hobbs, J. R., and Evans, D. A. (1980). Conversation as Planned Behavior. *Cognitive Science.* Vol. 4, No. 4.

Joshi, A. K., and Rosenschein, S. J. (1976). Some problems of inferencing: Relation of inferencing to decomposition of predicates. In *Proceedings of the International Conference on Computational Linguistics* (COLING 1976), Ottawa, Canada.

Joshi, A. K., and Weischedel, R. (1977). Computation of a subclass of inferences: Presupposition and entailment. *American Journal of Computational Linguistics.*

Kay, P. (1982). Three properties of the ideal reader. Department of Anthropology, University of California, Berkeley unpublished working paper.

Lehnert, W. (1978). *The Process of Question Answering.* Lawrence Erlbaum Associates, Hillsdale, N.J.

Marr, D. (1977). Artificial intelligence—A personal view. *Artificial Intelligence* 9, pp. 37–48.

McCarthy, J., and Hayes, P. (1969). Some philosophical problems from the standpoint of artificial intelligence. In B. Meltzer and D. Michie, (eds.), In *Machine Intelligence* Vol. 4, pp. 463–502. American Elsevier, New York.

McDermott, D. V. (1974). Assimilation of new information by a natural language-understanding system. MIT AI Laboratory TR-291.

McDermott, D. V. (1977). Flexibility and efficiency in a computer program for designing circuits. MIT AI Laboratory TR-402.

McDermott, D. V. (1980). Spatial inferences with ground, Metric formulas on simple objects. Yale University Computer Science Research Report #173.

Meehan, J. (1976). The metanovel: Writing stories by computer. Yale University Research Report #74.

Minsky, M. (1974). A framework for representing knowledge. MIT. AI Memo No. 306.

Miller, G. A., and Johnson-Laird, P. (1976). *Language and Perception.* Harvard University Press, Cambridge, Mass.

Moore, R. C. (1980). Reasoning about knowledge and action. Technical Note 191, SRI International Artificial Intelligence Center.

Newell, A., Shaw J. C., and Simon, H. A. (1959). Report on a general problem-solving program. In *Proceedings of the International Conference on Information Processing* (ICIP), Paris, UNESCO House.

Newell, A., and Simon, H. A. (1972). *Human Problem Solving.* Prentice-Hall, Englewood Cliffs, N.J.

Norman, D. A., and Rumelhart, D. E. (1975). *Explorations in Cognition.* W. H. Freeman and Co., San Francisco.

Perrault, C. R., and Cohen, P. R. (1977). Planning speech acts. AI-Memo 77-1, Department of Computer Science, Universiy of Toronto.

Perrault, C. R., Allen, J., and Cohen, P. R. (1978). Speech acts as basis for understanding dialogue coherence. *Proceedings of the Second Conference on Theoretical Issues in Natural Language Processing.* Champaigne-Urbana, Illinois.

Polti, G. (1916). *The Thirty-Six Dramatic Situations.* The Editor Company, Ridgewood, N.J.

Propp, V. (1968). *Morphology of the Folktale.* University of Texas Press, Austin.

Rich, C., and Shrobe, H. (1976). Initial report on a LISP programmer's apprentise. MIT AI Lab Technical Report 354.

Rieger, C. (1975a). Conceptual memory. In R. C. Schank (ed.), *Conceptual Information Processing.* North-Holland, Amsterdam.

Rieger, C. (1975b). The commonsense algorithm as a basis for computer models of human memory, inference, belief, and contextual language comprehension. In R. Schank and B. Webber (eds.), *Proceedings of the Conference on Theoretical Issues in Natural Language Processing.* Distributed by the Association for Computational Linguistics.

Riesbeck, C. K. (1976). Conceptual analysis. In R. C. Schank (ed.), *Conceptual Information Processing.* North-Holland, Amsterdam.

Riesbeck, C. K. and Schank, R. C. (1976). Comprehension by computer: Expectation-based analysis of sentences in context. Yale University Research Report #78.

Roberts, R., and Goldstein, I. (1977). NUDGE, A knowledge-based scheduling program. *Proceedings of the Fifth International Joint Conference on Artificial Intelligence.* Cambridge, Mass.

Roussel, P. (1975). Prolog: Manual de reference et d'utilisation. Technical Report, Groupe d'Intelligence Artificielle, Marseille-Luminy.

Rumelhart, D. E. (1976). Understanding and summarizing brief stories. Center for Human Information Processing Technical Report No. 58. University of California, San Diego.

Sacerdoti, E. D. (1974). Planning in a hierarchy of abstraction spaces. *Artificial Intelligence,* Vol. 5, No. 2, pp. 115–135.

Sacerdoti, E. D. (1977). *A Structure for Plans and Behavior.* Elsevier North-Holland, Amsterdam.

Schank, R. C. (1975). *Conceptual Information Processing.* North-Holland, Amsterdam.

Schank, R. C., and Abelson, R. P. (1977). *Scripts, Plans, Goals, and Understanding.* Lawrence Erlbaum Press, Hillsdale, N. J.

Schank, R. C., and Rieger, C. (1974). Inference and the computer understanding of natural language. *Artificial Intelligence* 5, pp. 373–412.

Schank, R. C., and Riesbeck, C. K. (1981). *Inside Computer Understanding: Five Programs Plus Miniatures.* Lawrence Erlbaum Associates, Hillsdale, N. J.

Schank, R. C., and Webber, B., editors. (1975). *Proceedings of the Conference on Theoretical Issues in Natural Language Processing.* Distributed by the Association for Computational Linguistics.

Schank, R. C., and Yale A. I. Project (1975). SAM—A story understander. Yale University Computer Sciences Reseach Report #43.

Schmidt, C. F., Sridharan, N. S., and Goodson, J. L. (1976). Recognizing plans and summarizing actions. *Proceedings of the Conference on Artificial Intelligence and the Simulation of Behavior.* pp. 291–306. Edinburgh, Scotland.

Schmidt, C. F., Sridharan, N. S., and Goodson, J. L. (1978). The plan recognition problem: An intersection of psychology and artificial intelligence. *Artificial Intelligence,* special issue on applications in the sciences and medicine.

Searle, John R. (1981). Minds, brains and programs. *The Behavorial and Brain Sciences.* Vol. 3, pp. 63–73.

Selfridge, O. G. (1959). Pandemonium: A Paradigm for Learning. *Proceedings of the Symposium on Mechanisation of Thought Processes.* 2 vols. National Physical Laboratory, Teddington, England. London: H. M. Stationary Office, 1959, pp. 511–529.

Shortliffe, E. H. (1974). MYCIN: A rule-based computer program for advising physicians regarding antimicrobial therapy selection. Stanford Artificial Intelligence Laboratory Memo AIM-251.

Stefik, M. (1980). Planning with contraints. Stanford Heuristic Programming Project HPP-80-12 (working paper).

Sussman, G. J. (1975). *A Computer Model of Skill Acquisition.* American Elsevier, New York.

Tate, A. (1975). Interacting goals and their use. *Proceedings of the Fourth International Joint Conference on Artificial Intelligence.* Tbilisi, Georgia, USSR.

Warren, D. H. D. (1974). WARPLAN: A system for generating plans. Department of Computational Logic, Memo No. 76, University of Edinburgh, Edinburgh.

Waterman, D. A. and Hayes-Roth, F. editors (1978). *Pattern-directed Inference Systems.* Academic Press, New York.

Wilensky, R. (1978). Understanding goal-based stories. Yale University Research Report #140.

Wilensky, R. (1980). Points: A theory of story content. Berkeley Electronic Research Laboratory Memorandum No. UCB/ERL/M8O/17.

Wilensky, R. (1981). Meta-planning: Representing and using knowledge about planning in problem solving and natural language understanding. *Cognitive Science.* Vol. 5, pp. 197–233.

Wilensky, R. (1982). Talking to UNIX in English: An Overview of UC. *Proceedings of the Second Annual National Conference on Artificial Intelligence.* Pittsburgh.

Wilensky, R., and Arens, Y. (1980). PHRAN: A knowledge-based approach to natural language analysis. Berkeley Electronic Research Laboratory Memorandum No. UCB/ERL/M8O/34.

Wilks, Y. (1977). Knowledge structures and language boundaries. In R. Schank and B. Webber (eds.), *Proceedings of the Conference on Theoretical Issues in Natural Language Processing.* Distributed by the Association for Computational Linguistics.

Wong, D. (1981). Language comprehension in a problem solver. In *Proceedings of the Seventh International Joint Conference on Artificial Intelligence.* Vancouver, British Columbia.

Zadeh, L. (1975). The concept of a linguistic variable and its application to approximate reasoning. *Information Sciences* 8 and 9, pp. 199–249, 301–357, 43–80.

Author Index

Author Index

Subject Index